AMERICAN
FOOTBALL

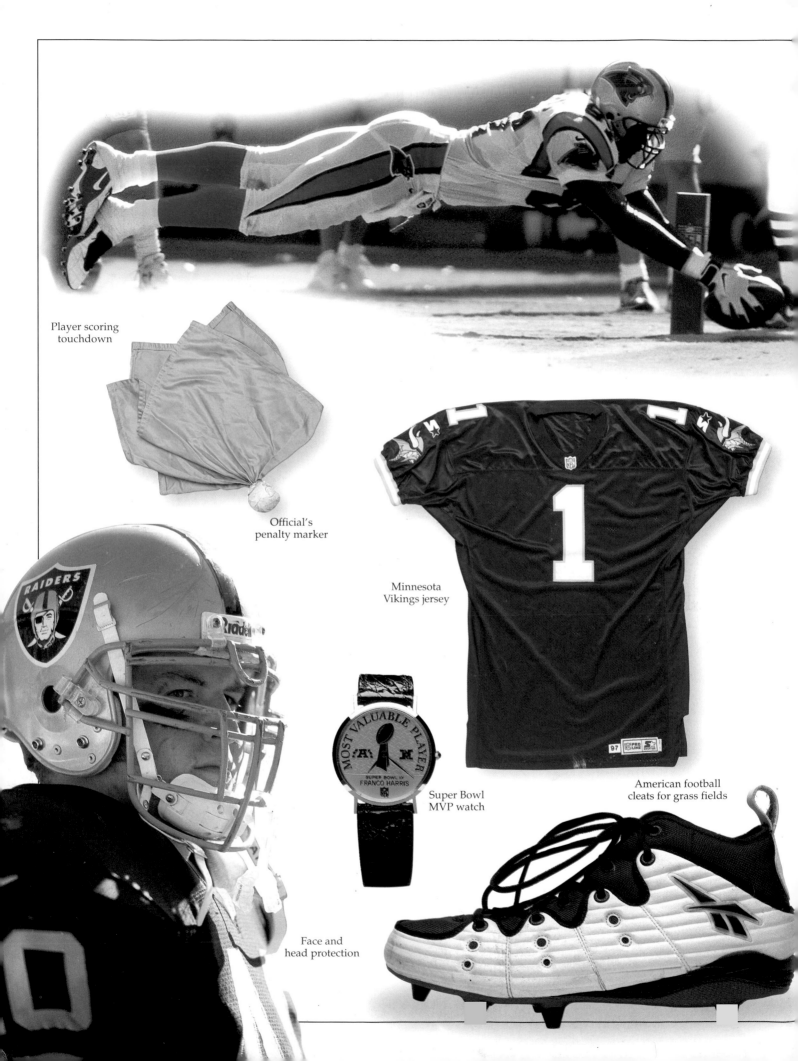

Player scoring
touchdown

Official's
penalty marker

Minnesota
Vikings jersey

Super Bowl
MVP watch

American football
cleats for grass fields

Face and
head protection

DK EYEWITNESS GUIDES

AMERICAN FOOTBALL

Created by
NFL PUBLISHING
Written by
JAMES BUCKLEY, JR.

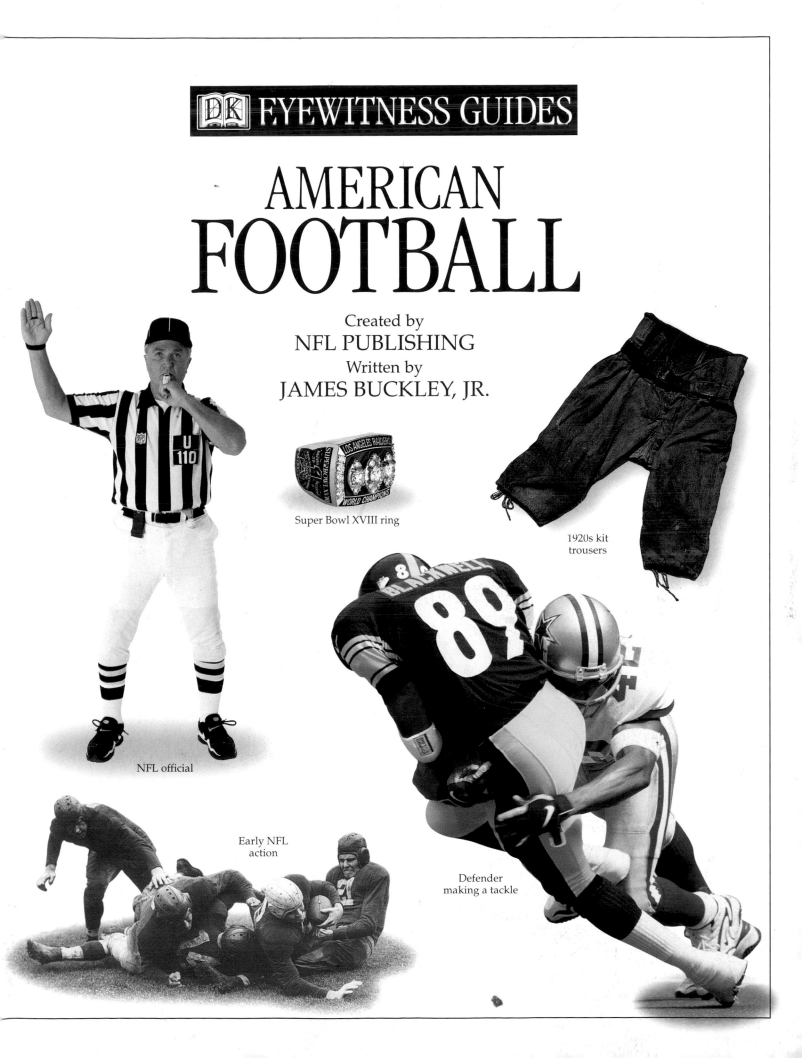

Super Bowl XVIII ring

1920s kit
trousers

NFL official

BLACKWELL 89

Early NFL
action

Defender
making a tackle

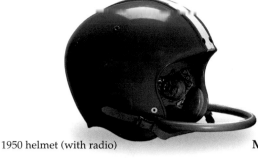

1950 helmet (with radio)

A Dorling Kindersley Book
www.dk.com

1909 football

Sideline yard marker

NFL PUBLISHING
Editor-in-Chief John Wiebusch
Managing Editor Chuck Garrity, Sr.
Project Art Director Bill Madrid
Project Editor James Buckley, Jr.
Director–Manufacturing Dick Falk
Director–Print Services Tina Dahl
Manager–Computer Graphics Sandy Gordon
Studio Photography Michael Burr

DORLING KINDERSLEY
Publisher Neal Porter
Executive Editor Iris Rosoff
Project Editor Constance Robinson
Art Director Dirk Kaufman

This Eyewitness ® Guide has been conceived by
Dorling Kindersley Limited and Editions Gallimard.

First published in Great Britain in 1999
by Dorling Kindersley Limited,
9 Henrietta Street, London WC2E 8PS
2 4 6 8 10 9 7 5 3

Copyright © 1999
Dorling Kindersley Limited, London
Text copyright © NFL Properties, Inc.

Super Bowl XXXII
programme cover

A CIP catalogue record for this book is available
from the British Library.

ISBN 0 7513 6302 2

Printed in China by Toppan Printing Co. (Shenzhen) Ltd.

VINCE LOMBARDI
TROPHY

NFL

Lombardi Trophy goes to
Super Bowl champion.

NOTE: American footballers measure distance in yards,
weight in pounds, and height in inches. Here is a
conversion chart to help you translate these
measurements into metres, kilograms,
and centimetres.

10 yards = 9 metres
200 pounds = 90 kilograms
6 feet = 1.8 metres
10 inches = 25.4 centimetres

Receiver
catching pass

Contents

How American Football Began

THE SPORT OF AMERICAN FOOTBALL has come a long way from its beginnings in the mid-19th century. American football grew out of English sports such as rugby and soccer and became popular on American college campuses in the late 1800s. But without pads or a recognized set of rules (and using a bulbous ball as shown right), football games usually were violent free-for-alls rather than organized athletic contests. In 1876, a coach named Walter Camp helped produce the first rules for American football. By the early 1900s, the game had grown in popularity and safety. College teams attracted national followings, and some fledgling local pro teams were formed. With innovations such as the forward pass, the game became more like the game as played today. The organization that became the National Football League was formed in 1920. From a rough-and-tumble beginning, American football has grown into an internationally loved sport played and watched by hundreds of millions of people.

DRESSING FOR THE GAME
Leather and canvas made up the bulk of the less-than-bulky equipment worn by players in football's early days. Sewn-in pads, as in the trousers and shoulders of this player from 1890, comprised the majority of the safety equipment. Players played bareheaded; the helmet was years away.

A NOSE FOR THE GAME
Safety equipment was rare. Only used by a few players, this nose protector was strapped around the head. A player held it in place by gripping it with his teeth.

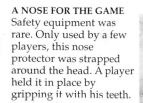

BRAWL IN THE FALL
The first recognized football game was played between Rutgers and Princeton universities in 1869, using rugby-like rules. This illustration, showing another game from that period, demonstrates the rough-and-tumble atmosphere. Also, notice the lack of any yard lines or end zones, as well as the vast expanse of the field. The 100-yard "gridiron" pattern for the field would not become standard until 1912.

Line item on season budget showing payment to Heffelfinger

PAY FOR PLAY
Amateurs and collegians dominated the early days of football; there were no true "professional" players. However, in 1892, former Yale star William (Pudge) Heffelfinger became the first recognized pro player when he accepted $500 (£316) to play for the Allegheny Athletic Association.

FOOTBALL: A TEAM GAME
After the turn of the century, semipro teams began to form in cities across the Midwest. In 1920, the Akron Pros, below, were the first champions of the first pro league, which later would become the NFL. Player/coach Fritz Pollard (far left) was one of several African-Americans to play pro football in the early years.

IT HAD LEGS
One part of football equipment that has remained strikingly unchanged are the trousers, which still fall to just below the knee and use a simple belt to hold them up. The high waist of these trousers from around 1900 protected the hips and lower back.

Finding an Audience

Until the NFL was formed in 1920, and for most of the decade afterward, college football was king. Universities such as Yale, Notre Dame, Minnesota, Washington, Southern California, Army, and Illinois attracted national attention while building championship teams. The NFL recognized this and began to recruit former college players, both to bolster their teams and to create publicity. The most famous college player, a man who attracted record crowds wherever he played, was University of Illinois star running back Harold (Red) Grange, the "Galloping Ghost". Spurred in part by the runaway success of Grange's professional career with the NFL's Chicago Bears and New York Yankees, the league grew in popularity with fans, especially in the Northeast and Midwest. NFL teams played in larger and larger stadiums to bigger and bigger crowds, tapping into and continuing the excitement first created by college teams.

"RED" GRANGE
CHICAGO BEARS
VS.
"BUCK" BAILEY
SAN FRANCISCO TIGERS

KEZAR STADIUM
Official Program

1926 exhibition game starred Red Grange

MR AMERICAN FOOTBALL
Red Grange was American football's first true superstar. Not only did his games attract record crowds – with Grange as the main attraction – he was among the first athletes to sign endorsements, such as these for sweets (above) and gum. He also starred in several movies.

SPORT KINGS GUM

RED GRANGE

GET YOUR PROGRAMMES!
The city of Canton, Ohio, home of the 1922-23 NFL-champion Bulldogs, holds a special place in NFL history. The site of the league's first organizational meeting and the home of the Pro Football Hall of Fame, the city symbolizes the NFL's midwestern roots.

CANTON BULLDOGS
WORLD CHAMPIONS

Price of this Program, Ten Cents

PERFECT MATCH

After Red Grange came players such as Earl (Dutch) Clark. Clark led the league in scoring three times, and helped the Detroit Lions win the 1935 NFL championship. He was among a handful of Hall of Fame players who helped the NFL continue its drive to the top of the sports world.

SAY CHEESE

Publicity is key to the success of any sports league. But the fast action on the field and the relative slowness of cameras of the era led to awkward posed shots, such as this one, that did not convey the true spirit and flavour of the game. However, they are still an important record of the NFL's early days.

MY HERO

As early as 1905, football players (such as Herman Kerckhoffe of the Massillon [Ohio] Football Club, above) were the object of worship by fans young and old.

THE NFL AND WWII

World War II slowed the growth of the league, as many players served with distinction overseas, including Medal of Honor winner Jack Lummus of the New York Giants. Back home, the league had grown enough to be used as a fund-raiser, as shown by this programme from a 1942 all-star game.

A BAND OF FANS

Showing a devotion they maintain to this day, fans of the Green Bay Packers formed a team band in the 1930s. As America's only community-owned sports club, the Packers remain a link to the NFL's scrappy early days.

Great Moments in NFL History

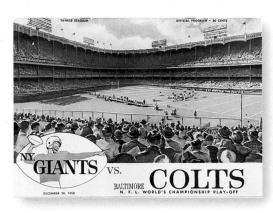

THE TAPESTRY THAT MAKES UP THE 80-YEAR HISTORY OF THE NFL includes heroes from the leather-helmet days of the 1920s; powerful championship teams from the 1950s; defining moments, such as the 1958 NFL Championship Game (left and below) or Super Bowl III; and enduring stars, a cavalcade that includes Red Grange, Otto Graham, Johnny Unitas, Jim Brown, Joe Namath, Walter Payton, Joe Montana, Emmitt Smith, John Elway, and many others. The stars of today follow in their footsteps, creating new memories – and more great moments – each Sunday in the autumn.

SUPER JOE
As cool under fire as he was talented, Joe Montana led the 49ers to four Super Bowl titles. He was the most valuable player in an NFL best three of those victories. Although he retired in 1994, Montana remains one of the most popular NFL players of all time.

73-0
The NFL has a few numbers that define history. One is 73-0, the score of the watershed 1940 NFL Championship Game, won by Chicago (in white above) over Washington. Redskins quarterback Sammy Baugh was asked afterwards if an early Washington touchdown might have made a difference: "Yes, it would have been 73-7".

GREATEST GAME
The Colts' thrilling 23-17 overtime victory over the Giants in the 1958 NFL Championship Game is sometimes called "The Greatest Game Ever Played". It was the first over-time game, and it was televised nationally. Millions of new NFL fans were created when Colts quarterback Johnny Unitas (19 at left) led his team on a stirring drive to a field goal that sent the game into overtime. Then he marched the team downfield to Alan Ameche's game-winning and league-defining touchdown.

BROADWAY JOE
If the 1958 championship game put the NFL on top, the Jets' victory in Super Bowl III assured that it would stay there. Quarter-back Joe Namath "guaran-teed" a victory, and, in one of sports' greatest upsets, made his boast stand up, defeating heavily favoured Baltimore 16-7.

SWEETNESS
Walter Payton (Chicago 1975-1987) ran for more yards – and with more style and grace – than any other NFL runner (through the 1998 season).

GREATEST SUPER BOWL EVER?
The Broncos' surprise victory in Super Bowl XXXII, 31-24 over the Packers, was a Super Bowl for the ages. A rousing back-and-forth battle between two great teams, it wasn't decided until the final play, which came 90 seconds after Terrell Davis (30) scored the winning touchdown on this short run.

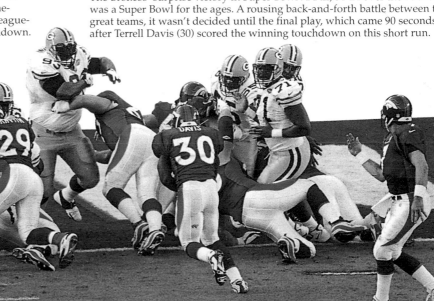

Inside the Football

THE DEFINITION OF A FOOTBALL IN THE NFL RULE BOOK gives little hint of the amazing things that NFL athletes do with it. The rules simply state that an NFL football "shall be made of an inflated rubber bladder enclosed in a pebble grained, leather case. It shall have the form of a prolate spheroid." While only a few football fans could identify the name of the shape of a football, most fans of any kind could identify a football itself. The streamlined oval shape of a football makes it perhaps the most recognizable ball in sports. Today's NFL ball is more tapered and pointed than the bulbous footballs used in the early days of the league. And, because home teams must provide 36 footballs ready for play at every game, the practice of using one ball for an entire game – no matter how beat up it became – also disappeared long ago. But no matter what goes into the making of a football, or what its shape is called, it is what NFL players *do* with the football that counts.

THE OLD 'PIGSKIN'

Time to correct a myth: footballs are made of leather, not pigskin. At the Wilson Football Factory in Ada, Ohio, which makes more than two million footballs of all sorts, every NFL ball begins life as four panels of water-resistant, specially tanned leather (left) that are stamped with company and league logos. After a synthetic lining is added, the four panels are stitched together inside out (below). Then holes are punched for laces.

Liner protects air bladder

Holes punched for laces

THE OFFICIAL FOOTBALL

Since 1954, Wilson Sporting Goods Company has supplied the NFL with all footballs for use in games. Each home team must supply 36 game balls (24 for indoor games) that are tested by the referee prior to kickoff. During the game, ball boys on the side of the field work with officials to place new balls into play. In bad weather, officials strive to provide clean and dry footballs to teams as well.

HANDS OF A GIANT

In the early days of the NFL, the football (above) was rounder and did not have the more pointed ends of today's ball. However, the basic shape, including lacing, already was established. The extra-large hands shown holding a 1930s football in this photograph belong to Pro Football Hall of Fame lineman Mel Hein of the New York Giants. For almost any player, even today, large hands come in handy when handling a football.

PERFECT FOR NIGHT GAMES

For a brief time in the 1950s, NFL teams experimented with white footballs during night games. At that time, NFL balls had stripes as well; the white ball had dark stripes, the brown ball white stripes. However, as stadium lighting improved, the need for a white ball decreased. The All-America Football Conference was the first to use the white football (the leagues merged in 1950, with three AAFC teams joining the NFL).

RIGHT SIDE OUT

The most difficult part of making a football comes next. Workers use skill, strength, and special tools to turn the sewn football panels right side out. This painstaking process is a practiced art, and only the most experienced turners work on NFL balls to ensure the highest quality product. Along with strong hands, these turners use steam boxes to warm and soften the leather, as well as a steel bar for leverage.

Area around holes for laces is double thickness.

Air bladder is inserted through opening.

LACE 'EM UP

After an air bladder is inserted, the football is ready to be laced up. Again, only the most experienced workers perform this important task on NFL footballs. The material for laces is called gridcord, and is made to withstand extremes in temperature.

NFL balls are double-laced.

All Shapes and Sizes

DO YOU HAVE TO BE HUGE TO PLAY IN THE NFL? Not necessarily. While size certainly is a factor, speed, skill, knowledge of the game, and courage are just as important. Look at Detroit running back Barry Sanders, who is second all-time in rushing yards and stands only 5 feet 8 inches tall. Or Atlanta kick returner Tim Dwight, 5–8 and 184 pounds, who returned a kick-off 94 yards for a touchdown in Super Bowl XXXIII. But there are giants in the NFL. More and more players are like Jacksonville's Pro Bowl offensive tackle Tony Boselli, who is 6–7 and weighs 325 pounds – much larger than linemen from the early days of the NFL (see growth chart). It is not unusual for the offensive linemen on a typical NFL team to average nearly 300 pounds. You do not have to be a giant to play football. But it doesn't hurt.

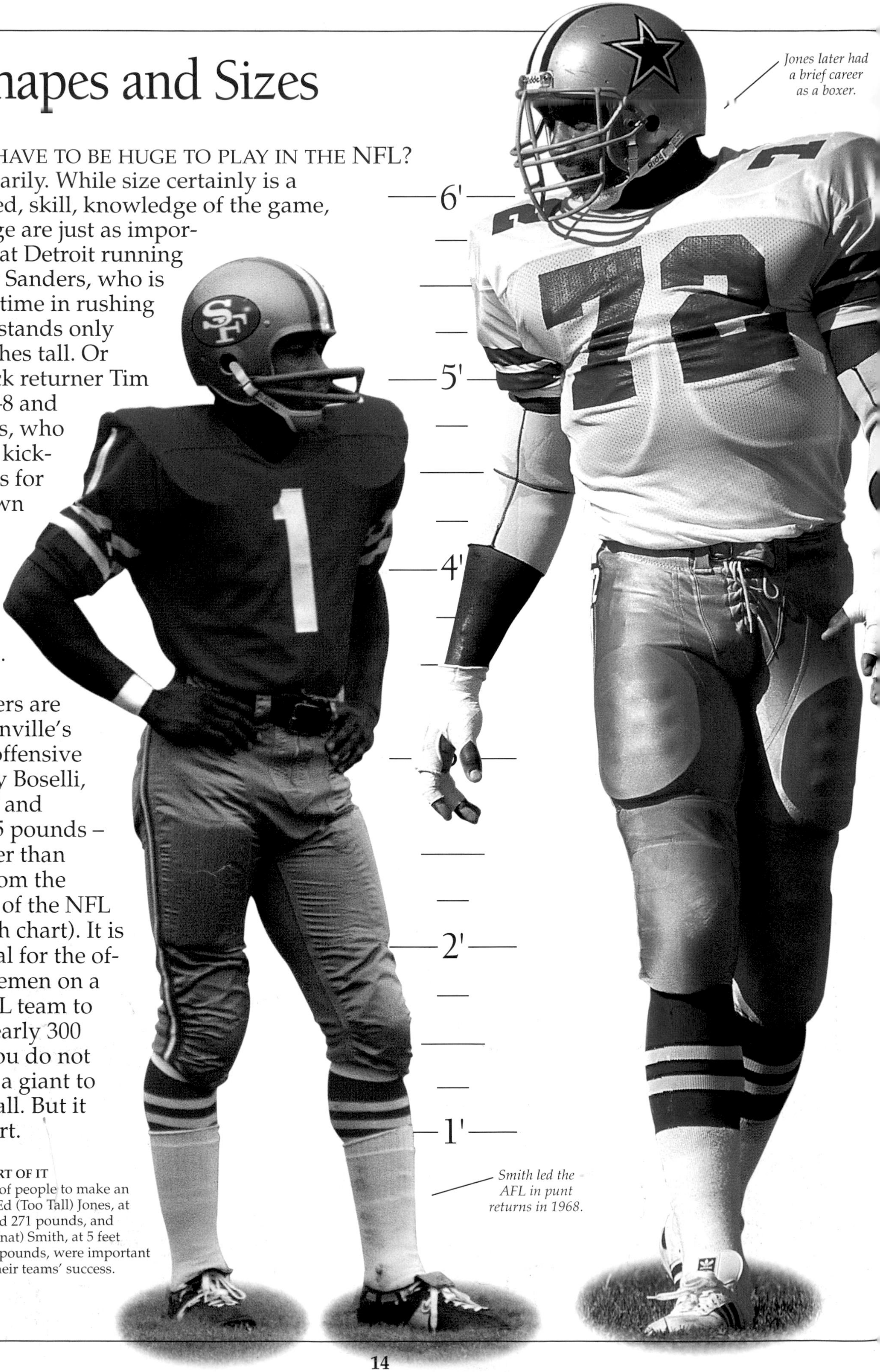

LONG AND SHORT OF IT
It takes all kinds of people to make an NFL team. Both Ed (Too Tall) Jones, at 6 feet 9 inches and 271 pounds, and Noland (Super Gnat) Smith, at 5 feet 4 inches and 154 pounds, were important contributors to their teams' success.

— 6' —

— 5' —

— 4' —

— 2' —

— 1' —

Jones later had a brief career as a boxer.

Smith led the AFL in punt returns in 1968.

14

1935: Mel Hein, 6–1, 234 pounds

1955: Lou Groza, 6–2, 243 pounds

1976: Art Shell, 6–4, 261

1999: Tony Boselli, 6–7, 325

GROWING UP
NFL players have gotten bigger as the game has gotten bigger. The top three players pictured left – all members of the Pro Football Hall of Fame – represent the average size of offensive linemen from their respective eras. Boselli, at bottom, is among the largest NFL players today; he is about 3 inches and 20 pounds bigger than average. The factors that have helped athletes grow over the years include improved year-round training techniques, better nutrition and coaching, and lighter, yet stronger, gear.

BIG GUYS IN THE MIDDLE
Girth can mean greatness on the line of scrimmage. Just ask former Pro Bowl players Gilbert Brown (345 pounds, left) and Nate Newton (320 pounds).

THIN MEANS WIN
While linemen need weight to make them effective, quarterbacks such as Randall Cunningham (left) and wide receivers often are slender and have greater mobility and speed. However, they also must be strong to evade tacklers and absorb hits.

BIG AND LITTLE
Teammates of all sizes work together to win. Detroit's offensive line (right) towers over running back Barry Sanders (20). While he depends on them to open holes, they depend on him to advance the ball and reach the end zone.

The Football Field

THE FIRST FOOTBALL FIELDS were just that – fields. Games were played in large open spaces near Eastern college campuses. The dimensions were determined more by buildings, barns, and roads than by a rule book. As the game grew in popularity, the need for a standard-sized field was recognized. By 1912, a 100-yard field with 10-yard end zones was the norm. Field markings, including yard-line numbers, hashmarks, and yardage stripes, have changed over time as the game and technology have evolved. The markings are used by players and officials on the field and by spectators – those watching in the stands and on television – to keep track of the movement of the ball up and down the field. A football field also is known as a gridiron; early football fields were drawn with a cross-hatch grid of lines to aid officials.

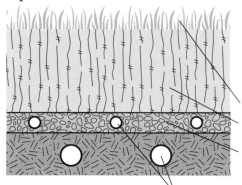

Grass

Root zone (dirt)

Gravel

Drainage and irrigation pipes

UNDER THE FIELD
Today's high-tech NFL fields are made of more than meets the eye. Several layers of materials are built up to support, drain, and preserve the playing surface. The grass at many stadiums is changed annually.

NFL fields are 53⅓ yards wide.

Yard lines span the width of the field every 5 yards.

UNDER A ROOF
In 1932, many years before domed stadiums were built, the first indoor NFL game was played in Chicago Stadium. Bitter cold forced the game to be played indoors on a modified 80-yard field. Hashmarks, used for the first time for safety, became standard in the NFL the next season.

One-yard increments are marked along each sideline.

Ten-yard-deep end zones are located at opposite ends of the field

Steelers

SIDELINE STUFF
Bright orange yard markers are placed every 10 yards along both sidelines to aid players and fans. The foot-high markers are made of foam rubber for the players' safety. The large "G" denotes the goal line. Four vertical foam-rubber pylons (below) mark the corners of each end zone.

30

G

NFL NFL

Pylons, which denote the boundaries of the end zone, are considered part of the playing field.

Large yard markers are placed every 10 yards.

An orange ribbon atop each post helps kickers gauge wind direction and strength.

The bench area (blue and white) is reserved for players, coaches, and staff.

IT'S UP...IT'S GOOD!
Kickers aim field-goal and extra-point attempts at the 18-foot 6-inch span between the two 30-foot high goal posts. The cross-bar is 10 feet off the ground. In 1974, the goal posts were moved from the front to the back of the end zone.

The out-of-bounds area is marked by a six-foot-wide white border

NFL teams use a variety of logos to decorate their fields.

Hashmarks are located 70 feet 9 inches from each sideline. The ball is placed on or between them to start play.

Goal posts are located at the back centre of each end zone.

How to Tell Who's Who

LIKE KNIGHTS OF OLD, NFL players stride into action wearing insignia and colours that tell the world whom they represent. The symbols on their uniforms and helmets identify players by their team's location and its nickname. In the half-century since the first NFL helmet was painted with a logo (right), the distinctive logos, colours, and mascots of pro football teams have become more than simple identifying marks. They are the focus of a whole industry built around team-identified merchandise. To fans, the logos are more than just ornamentation; logos represent the sport they love, the teams they support, and the tradition they cherish.

Yellow paint on blue-painted helmet

THE BEGINNING OF A TREND
The first NFL team to sport any sort of ornamentation on its helmets was the Rams. In 1948, Rams halfback Fred Gehrke, who majored in art in college, painted these ram horns on the team's helmets. With only slight modifications, the design remains the team's symbol today.

MAKING A SPLASH
In the early days of NFL Europe, then known as the World League, teams wore uniforms with vibrant colours and wild patterns. They were more modern art than modern football, and have been replaced by more traditional designs.

THROWBACKS
In 1994, NFL teams celebrated the league's 75th anniversary by wearing replicas of old uniform styles. The Broncos' John Elway wore a jersey that was modelled after the style Denver wore in 1963.

18

Buccaneers
Cardinals
Chargers
Chiefs

Colts
Cowboys
Dolphins
Eagles
Falcons
Forty-Niners
Giants
Jaguars

 Jets

 Lions

 Packers

 Panthers

 Patriots

 Raiders

 Rams

 Ravens

 Redskins

 Saints

 Seahawks

 Steelers

 Titans

 Vikings

MEN IN BLACK (AND WHITE)

The seven game officials dress in white trousers and black-and-white striped shirts. The pattern is used to avoid confusion with any teams' jerseys.

Heavy-duty logo sticker

STICKY STUFF

The helmet displays the team's logo most prominently, so teams make a good presentation. Before each game, helmets are cleaned and polished by the equipment staff. New logo stickers are affixed when needed (Saints, above).

"STEEL" UNIQUE

The meaning of most NFL logos is obvious: a lion, a ram, a dolphin, a Viking. The Pittsburgh Steelers' logo, however, demands an explanation. The three star-like shapes are called hypocycloids, and represent the three elements of steel produced in the city, as well as Pittsburgh's three rivers.

Each official also has a unique uniform number; the "R" is for referee.

All-leather helmet from 1948

Referees wear white hats; all other officials wear black hats.

NEW STYLE

Uniform changes seemed to help the Broncos. In 1997, their first season in these dark-blue jerseys with orange trim, the team won its first Super Bowl. Other teams in recent years, including the Jets and Buccaneers, have improved during their first season in new uniforms.

OLD STYLE

As fashions change, uniforms change. Many teams have updated their uniforms over the years. Here John Elway models the orange and bright-blue model worn by the Broncos from 1968-1996.

The Coaches

H E NEVER CATCHES A PASS. He does not return kickoffs, block punts, or make tackles. But the decisions he makes, during the offseason, before kickoff, and during every game, often can mean the difference between victory and defeat. He is the head coach of an NFL team, and the buck stops with him. Today's NFL coach, assisted by coaches for every position, has the ultimate responsiblity for the success or failure of his team. Most head coaches are heavily involved in selecting players for their rosters; they determine which players will start; they devise formations and strategies to defeat each opponent. Head coaches lead, inspire, teach, cajole, encourage, yell, pat on the back – whatever it takes to form a winning team out of a group of individuals.

Coaches often ride blocking sleds to observe technique and offer encouragement.

Head coaches communicate with assistants via special radios.

PRACTICE MAKES PERFECT
Game day is the briefest part of an NFL coach's week on the job. His routine includes, among many other things, game planning, practice scheduling, running practice, working with players individually and in groups, scouting opponents, and, occasionally, sleeping.

Special field credentials identify team personnel to stadium security.

Head coaches can switch channels on their radios to talk to offensive or defensive assistants.

PURPLE, GOLD, AND GREEN
As if Dennis Green was not busy enough as head coach of the Minnesota Vikings, he also contributes his expertise to the league's Competition Committee, which oversees on-field play and rules changes. He is joined on that committee by Seattle head coach Mike Holmgren and Pittsburgh head coach Bill Cowher.

Headsets link to coaches on sidelines.

PLAY TIME Players are expected to memorize play diagrams used in practice and games. But coaches (right) always are ready to demonstrate plays again and again.

COACHES'-EYE VIEW
More than ever before, players and coaches on the sidelines rely on the eagle eyes of coaches sitting in special booths above the playing field. From this perspective, coaches get a wider vision of the field and can use direct radio and telephone links to help on-field coaches decide on the best strategies to win.

OKAY, HERE'S WHAT I WANT YOU TO DO
Coaches work with players between series to explain what went right and how to repeat it, or what went wrong and how to fix it. Coaches combine paper diagrams, erasable white boards, and still photos from video cameras above the field with their own particular styles of vocalization to get their points across.

FOUR LEGENDS Among them, these four innovative and influential Pro Football Hall of Fame head coaches represent nearly every era of NFL champions: Halas in the 1930s and 1940s, Brown in the 1940s and 1950s, Lombardi in the 1960s, and Walsh in the 1980s.

Paul Brown, Browns and Bengals

Vince Lombardi, Packers and Redskins; George Halas, Bears

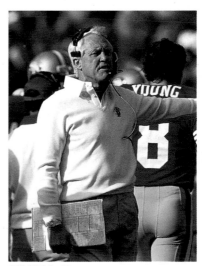

Bill Walsh, 49ers

The American Football Helmet

THE MOST DISTINCTIVE piece of Amercian football equipment is the helmet. It also is the most important element of safety equipment because it protects the player's head and face from the collisions and contact that occur throughout a game. Early NFL players wore no helmets. Leather helmets came into wide use in the 1930s and 1940s, but they afforded little protection and did not cover the face. Using technology developed for American soldiers' helmets during World War II, NFL players began to wear hard plastic helmets surrounding canvas suspension belts; protective facemasks were added soon after. Helmets used in the NFL today combine high-tech plastics, inflatable, form-fitting air bladders, and a multitude of adjustable straps to create the safest helmet possible.

Crown inflation valve

Warning labels

Earhole

*Chin strap
(usually paired)*

Riddell

EARLY DAYS
When early NFL and college football players wore helmets at all, they were flimsy leather caps, sometimes with ear flaps. They were so pliable that they could be folded and carried in pockets.

MORE UP TOP
More padding was added to the top of helmets in the 1920s. Occasionally teams added colour as a team identifier. However, the simple color schemes were a far cry from today's NFL helmets.

GETTING AHEAD
Rawlings Sporting Goods produced the first moulded hard-leather helmet in the 1930s; some were covered by a fabric shell. By 1940, every NFL player wore a helmet, many like this one, the Zuppke Varsity Model.

ATOP THE ROMAN HEAD

Warfare, not sports, has been the main use of helmets throughout history. This Roman helmet used by legions in ancient Gaul was worn as much to frighten opponents as protect soldiers.

STATUS SEEKER

Medieval knights used their metal helmets for protection and to announce their status and allegiance, much as NFL players' helmets and facemask styles signify team and position.

A PIECE OF WAR

Though made of steel, not plastic, American World War II soldiers' "pots" inspired John Riddell to create the plastic suspension helmets that would become standard in the NFL for years.

Facemask clips

Externally inflatable crown pads

THE AIR UP THERE

Today's helmets rely not only on materials such as polycarbonate Lexan for strength, they use air bladders for cushioning. This cutaway view (without facemask) shows the bladders and pads that fully surround the head on the top and sides, individually moulding to each players' head shape.

Occipital pad

Facemask

Side air bladders

Chin strap cup

WE'LL PUMP YOU UP

NFL equipment managers use hand pumps during games to ensure that helmet liners and pads are fully inflated for maximum safety and protection.

Externally inflatable back/neck/side liner

Snap-in jaw pad

AHEAD OF THE GAME

By 1950, light – yet strong – plastic helmets had been perfected. This particular short-lived model from 1956 had a radio used by the quarterback to receive signals. It didn't work well then, but today such technology is standard in the NFL.

LEATHERHEADS

Pro Football Hall of Fame running back Bronko Nagurski of the Chicago Bears (1930-37, 1943) models a leather helmet. The primitiveness of early NFL equipment bred tough players, such as Nagurski, who probably would scoff at today's safer, high-tech gear.

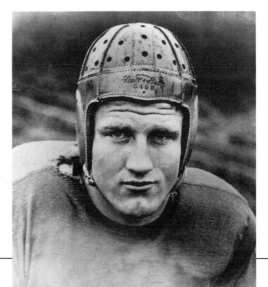

Face Protection

THE FIRST FOOTBALL PLAYERS FACED THEIR OPPONENTS nose to nose – literally. There was little or no protective gear for players' faces, including this rare leather mask (right). Players learned tackling and blocking techniques that helped them avoid face-smashing situations. But they couldn't avoid all of them. As helmets improved in quality and strength, facemasks were attached to protect jaws, noses, and faces. The first facemasks were crude metal bars. Later, some facemasks took the form of a plastic band. As the modern, hard-plastic helmet evolved, a cage-like facemask of rubber-covered steel became the standard. Today, NFL players use masks that let them do their jobs while giving them the greatest protection. Linemen have larger facemasks with more bars. Quarterbacks, running backs, and other players who handle the ball wear smaller facemasks for better visibility.

Double chin straps for extra stability

Rounded metal bars

Vertical and horizontal bars provide protection and stability.

Hard plastic chin strap has padded liner.

Mouth guards are individually moulded for each player.

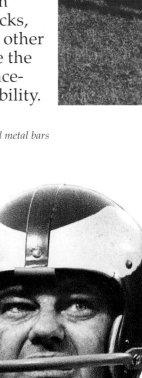

SINGLE BARS
Early metal facemasks were simple round bars. This style, shown here on Pro Football Hall of Fame quarterback Norm Van Brocklin, quickly proved to be inadequate. Today, only a few kickers wear single bars.

ANOTHER KIND OF BLACK EYE
Beneath their masks, some players add an additional layer of protection. Eye black absorbs bright sunlight and reduces glare. Some players smear on a greasy substance; others use special pieces of black tape.

PLASTIC MAN
Bands of acrylic briefly were tried out as facemasks by some teams in the 1950s. As Y.A. Tittle (14) and other players learned, this breakable material was not up to the rough-and-tumble life of the NFL.

MORE IS BETTER
Facemasks that attached across the entire front of the helmet became the standard. Additional bars were added for further protection. Hall of Fame linebacker Bobby Bell wore this version in 1969.

SAVING FACE
Today's modern facemasks offer the greatest protection yet. Some players have added plastic visors to keep unwanted fingers out of their eyes. Note that the shaded version on the left can be worn only with special permission, for safety reasons.

Safety First

Without the proper training and protection, football can be a dangerous game. In fact, in the early part of the century, before the NFL came along, President Theodore Roosevelt threatened to ban the sport in response to some deaths. However, as the NFL grew, the desire to protect its players from the rigours of the game grew as well. Using the latest materials and technology available, each generation has created new methods of protection. Early NFL players used only leather pads and helmets, leather being the strongest material available. After World War II, strong and lightweight plastic materials were developed that changed the way players were protected. Shoulder pads became lighter and more flexible, yet safer than before. Foam padding replaced cotton stuffing, reducing weight while increasing strength. Today's advanced protective equipment, combined with improved training and rehabilitation techniques, makes football as safe as it possibly can be for players.

Neck padding

Laces tie the two halves of the pads together.

GIVING THEM THE OLD SHOULDER
Leather and canvas were the main components of these early shoulder pads. The hard leather pads on top were cushioned underneath with canvas pads, but still were weighty and unwieldy. Before these removable pads came into use in the 1940s, players relied on jerseys with thin pads sewn into the tops of the shoulders.

MOUTH OFF
All NFL players are required to wear mouth guards. Before each season, a team dentist creates a rubber mouth guard individually moulded to each player's teeth. Most players take the mouth guard out between plays. The helmet strap keeps the mouth guard handy.

PADDED SHOULDERS

Along with the helmet, shoulder pads are among the most recognizable pieces of football equipment. The pads help give the NFL player his distinctive, broad-shouldered look. More importantly, shoulder pads are one of the players' most important protective devices.

Outer shell is hard plastic.

Elastic straps keep the pads from sliding.

Leather straps and metal buckles cinch the pads tightly around the player's chest.

HANDS DOWN

Offensive linemen often wear padded gloves such as these. Receivers and running backs sometimes wear thinner gloves that give them a good feel for the ball. In today's NFL, quarterbacks are among the few players who do not wear some type of glove.

STRAPPING IN

Players sometimes need assistance tightening and adjusting their shoulder pads for the best and safest fit. An equipment manager (right) learns each player's particular fit needs and stands ready to help them get ready for games and practices. Notice how tightly this lineman's jersey fits over his shoulder pads. This is to prevent defenders from grabbing his jersey.

Ridges help keep pads from slipping.

Pad is contoured to fit snugly over the players' kneecaps.

HEAVY THIGH

The dense foam-rubber thigh pad takes nearly as much punishment as the shoulder pads. Players wear these pads in special pockets in the legs of their uniform trousers.

ELBOWING IN

Some players choose to use elbow pads. A cloth cover surrounds a foam-rubber pad. A wide elastic strap (other side, not shown) keeps the pad in place on the player's arm.

KNEE HIGH

Nearly all players wear these thin foam-rubber knee pads inside pockets in their uniform trousers. These pads are very flexible to allow the player complete freedom of movement.

Kitted Out

THERE IS AN OLD SPORTS SAYING: "You can't tell the players without a scorecard." While that may be true, an NFL player's kit number is the real way to tell who he is. The earliest football kits were simple scarves or cloths worn around a player's waist. As organized teams were formed, distinctive team kits were created, though teams could do only so much with the heavy wool jerseys of the day. Some of the more distinctive logos on early NFL jerseys included the interlocked C's of the Chicago Cardinals and the black-and-white igloo of the Duluth Eskimos. Today's NFL kits are made from strong, lightweight, colourful fabrics decorated with some of the most recognizable logos and numbers in sports. But no matter what the jersey is made of or what logo is on it, any NFL player will tell you that putting on his team jersey changes him from a man into an athlete on a mission.

Orange stripes on navy blue jerseys

BEAR SUITS
Chicago Bears founder, coach, and player George Halas (left) and teammate Ed (Dutch) Sternaman show off their Bears kits from the 1920s.

GETTING STARTED
Early NFL jerseys were made of heavy wool that became even heavier with sweat, rain, or snow. While most teams favored muted colours, the Canton Bulldogs (left), wore maroon from 1920-27. Many early NFL teams provided only jerseys; the players were responsible for supplying other parts of their kits.

Some players wore heavy canvas gloves.

28

Smaller numbers are placed on top of the shoulders or on the sleeves.

Style of front laces remains virtually unchanged from early days of NFL.

A TIGHT FIT
NFL trousers once were made of heavy canvas and leather. Today, Lycra and Spandex are used to create trousers that are durable yet comfortable and very pliable. Players wear them very tightly both for comfort and to avoid giving defenders anything to grab. One thing that hasn't changed much over the years is the trousers' basic design.

Area covering shoulder pads is double thickness.

Numbers must be at least eight inches high and four inches wide, and of a sharply contrasting colour.

Side gusset lets jersey stretch when player twists or turns.

NFL seal of authenticity

NFL shield appears in the same place on all teams' trousers.

TEARAWAYS
For a few years in the 1970s and 1980s, NFL jerseys were made of a material that ripped easily. These "tearaway" jerseys gave offensive players an edge, leaving would-be tacklers holding nothing but a handful of shirt as their opponent escaped.

SHIRT OFF HIS BACK
NFL jerseys are made of one hundred per cent nylon, a strong yet pliable material. A pattern of ventilation holes helps keep players cool and dry in the heat of a game. The shoulders are extra wide to allow room for shoulder pads.

Elastic around knees keeps trousers snug.

NEVERS ON SUNDAY
Most early NFL teams did not have any sort of logo or mark on their kit jerseys. An exception was the Duluth Eskimos (1926-27), who sported an igloo on the front of their jerseys. This illustration shows Eskimos star Ernie Nevers. In 1929, Nevers, while with the Chicago Cardinals, scored an NFL-record 40 points in one game.

Getting Ready for Game Day

A KNIGHT PUTTING ON HIS ARMOUR. A firefighter pulling on his gear. These are a couple of the classic metaphors used to describe an NFL player getting ready to play a game. Preparation for the game is as much mental as physical. Each piece of a player's equipment goes on in a certain order. Each piece has a role in helping protect a player and helping him do his job. But as a player goes through the routine of putting on pads, trousers, jersey, and helmet, he is putting on mental armour, too. He goes over the plays he will need for the day's game. He sets his mind to the physical task ahead. He steels his will to wear his jersey with pride and to do everything he must to win. The kit and pads he wears are the costume for his role as an NFL player. It is up to him to play that part to the best of his ability.

PADS IN TROUSERS
Players slip thigh and knee pads into special pockets in the legs of their kit trousers. Many players stretch out, put on their trousers, then stretch out to ensure a snug and comfortable fit.

UP ON TOP
After more stretching, players put on and tighten their shoulder pads. Some players, including linemen, put on their shoulder pads and jerseys as a unit to ensure a tight fit.

NEW JERSEY
According to NFL rules, jerseys must remain tucked into trousers during the game. At this point, players are making final adjustments to the fit of their trousers and jersey.

UNDER IT ALL
NFL players wear a variety of undergarments beneath their kits, ranging from T-shirts to compression shorts that help prevent muscle pulls.

Straps and buckles tighten around chest.

Thigh and knees pads are placed in pockets.

Hip pads are tucked into trousers.

Socks are white on bottom, team colour on top.

Shoes are put on before shoulder pads.

Belt is tightened last.

Trousers are held up with laces and belt.

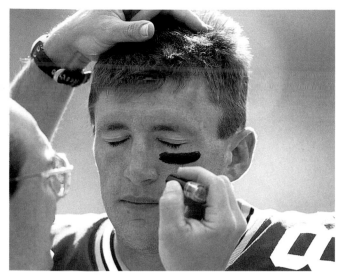

ONE LAST THING
On sunny days, a swatch of eye black can help absorb glaring rays. Equipment managers help players apply the eye black using a tube not unlike one used for lipstick or lip balm.

FINAL TOUCHES
Every player must wear shoulder pads. But there is some optional protective gear, such as elbow pads, padded gloves, neck rolls, and forearm pads, that players can use if they want.

Elbow pads

Jersey must fully cover shoulder pads.

Helmet ready for use

READY FOR INSPECTION
The NFL has numerous kit rules to ensure the players' safety; all players also must have similar equipment. The umpire is the official in charge of detecting and correcting any kit violations. Once the game begins, the equipment manager works constantly with players to ensure that their equipment and kit are in good order. Shoelaces can break, gloves can rip, jerseys can be torn; whatever problem happens, the equipment manager's trunk has the solution.

Padded gloves

Footwear

IF A FOOTBALL PLAYER'S LEGS ARE THE ENGINE that makes him go, then his feet are the wheels. NFL players need sturdy, supportive footwear to withstand the pounding of a game. Football shoes worn on grass surfaces are known as cleats, after the screw-in plastic studs on the bottoms of the soles. These cleats help a player dig into the turf for a strong forward push at the line of scrimmage. Cleats also help players turn instantly to dodge tacklers. Although cleats have been a part of football shoes since the early days, it was not until the 1920s that replaceable screw-in cleats came into use; until then cleats were tacked to the soles. Then, as now, leather was the key component of football shoes. Good in all weather, leather is tough enough, yet flexible enough, to perform well in football. Today, however, nylon and other materials combine with leather to form colourful football shoes that are both lightweight and strong.

Square toe for kicking

Dozens of small rubber nubs help players grip the artificial turf.

ARTIFICIAL TURF SHOES
Some outdoor NFL stadiums, and all indoor stadiums, have artificial turf fields. Instead of grass, the playing surface is a material made of varying brands of a spongy plastic-and-rubber-like material. Instead of traditional football cleats that would not dig into the artificial turf, players wear shoes with special rubber soles such as these.

'THE TOE'
Pro Football Hall of Fame member Lou (The Toe) Groza (above) demonstrates how to use the square-toed kicking shoe. In Groza's day, kickers did more than kick; Groza was a star lineman as well as a kicker for field goals and extra points. Groza's shoes had to function as both regular football cleats and be used in the toe-first kicking style.

REALLY BIG SHOES
These size 13 (UK size 12) football cleats, worn by San Francisco 49ers linemen, are shown actual size. Not surprisingly, football cleats come in very large sizes to support the big men who wear them. One of the largest pair belonged to Cincinnati's Willie Anderson, who wore a size 19 shoe.

The lower half of this shoe is leather; the upper is heavy-duty nylon.

Holes for ventilation

Shorter or longer cleats can be used, depending on field conditions.

Extra cushions in heels reduce stress on feet.

ANTIQUE CLEATS

These leather football shoes date to the 1930s and were among the first models with screw-in cleats. However, they were much heavier than football shoes of today, with thicker leather soles and heavy leather uppers. Some players today wear a style of "high top" shoes similar to these for better ankle support.

SHOELESS TOMMY

Many kickers and punters use special kicking shoes that are made of lighter leather than shoes used by other players. San Diego punter Darren Bennett still uses shoes he first used in the Australian Football League. And then there are the players who do not bother with a kicking shoe at all. San Francisco's Tommy Thompson (left) was one of several players who kicked or punted barefoot.

Heavy-duty laces

Thick nylon-covered pads help keep the shoe snug around the ankles.

Moving the Ball

THE OBJECT OF THE GAME is to move the football downfield – and as a result, score points. On offence, teams move the ball two ways: running and passing. Running plays involve the quarterback handing off or pitching the ball to a running back, who runs downfield behind his blockers. On passing plays, the quarterback throws the ball to a teammate. However, those simple descriptions do not begin to explain the many ways that teams put those plays into action. Running plays can go through the middle of the line or sweep around the ends. There can be multiple handoffs. Even the quarterback can run with the ball. Passing plays can be long or short, from simple flares to the outside to long "bombs" many yards downfield.

TOUCHDOWN!
That is the aim of every offensive play, and the result of this spectacular one by the Carolina Panthers (above). The ball must cross the plane of the goal line to count as a touchdown. Players can carry the ball into the end zone from the field or catch it while in the end zone.

ON THE RUN
Most NFL teams today run slightly less often than they pass. The goal of most running plays is less ambitious than most passing plays. Top runners, such as Detroit's Barry Sanders (right) gain from 4 to 5 yards per carry, as compared to 7-8 yards and up averaged on pass plays. However, running plays more often go for positive yardage, while only about half of attempted passes are completed.

Defensive team

GETTING STARTED
Every offensive play begins at the "line of scrimmage", an imaginary line that crosses the width of the field. The offence and defence must remain on opposite sides of this line until the ball is "snapped," or thrown backward from the ground to the quarterback. At the snap, each team surges forward trying to gain the advantage of momentum. The line of scrimmage has its origins in the rug-by scrum.

PASSING FANCY

Dan Marino of the Dolphins – who holds many NFL career records, including passing yards, touchdown passes, and completions – demonstrates the fine art of passing a football. The keys to success include setting the feet, pointing the front shoulder at the target, and following through across the body. While every quarterback has a slightly different passing style, they share the same goal: deliver the ball quickly and accurately to a teammate down the field.

Pylon marks goal line

FIRST AND 10

An offensive team has four "downs", or plays, to move the ball 10 yards. If it does not, it must give the ball to the other team. Talking football: after a gain of 3 yards, the next play is "second and 7." Down markers help teams and fans keep track of the "down".

Goal line

Center "snaps" the ball to the quarterback

Offensive team (with ball)

Line of scrimmage centred between the two teams

BOMBS AWAY!

Few plays in football are more exciting than a long pass down-field. A sprinting receiver runs underneath a rainbow pass that can travel more than 60 yards in the air. Randy Moss of the Vikings (right) made 10 touchdown catches of 50 yards or more in 1998. However, most pass plays are much shorter and are designed for gaining chunks of yardage rather than scoring.

Contact Sport

A FOOTBALL GAME HAS MOMENTS OF PURE GRACE: a diving reception, a field-spanning run, a perfectly thrown spiral. But between the grace notes comes the sharp crack of contact. On offence, the object of the game is to score, and to do that blockers must knock defenders out of the way. On defence, the object is to stop opponents from scoring; contact is the means to that end. NFL players are well-protected by the latest in safety gear, and they are well-schooled in safe tackling and blocking techniques. But no matter how thick the pads or perfect the tackles, a collision between a big defensive lineman and a medium-size running back or between a tough safety and a high-flying receiver is dramatic proof that this is a contact sport. NFL players are some of the toughest athletes in the world. They have to be – they play one of the toughest sports.

A clean tackle leads with the shoulder, not the helmet.

FIRST CONTACT
At the snap of the ball, the offensive and defensive linemen collide with a collective grunt. A blocker (77) can push and shove, but not grab a defender (92) to make room for the play.

'TWAS EVER THUS
In the early days of the NFL, the helmets were leather and the pads were thinner, but the contact was just as fierce.

UP AND OVER

A receiver who leaps to make a catch may not know on which end he will land. Spectacular midair collisions are part of the game, though, and NFL players become experts in the art of falling safely.

SACKED!

Sacked usually means you have been fired from your job. In the NFL, it means it is time for a defensive player (in blue) to celebrate making a big play – tackling the quarterback (in white) behind the line of scrimmage.

CLEAN TACKLE

A defender's most useful skill is tackling. That is, stopping the player with the ball by knocking him to the ground or pushing him out of bounds. This Dallas defender shows good form in tackling a Pittsburgh receiver after a catch. Defenders are taught to "drive through" an opponent, using leverage and weight to stop the runner's forward progress and end the play.

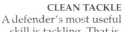

Defenders try to "wrap up" ball carriers for a sure tackle.

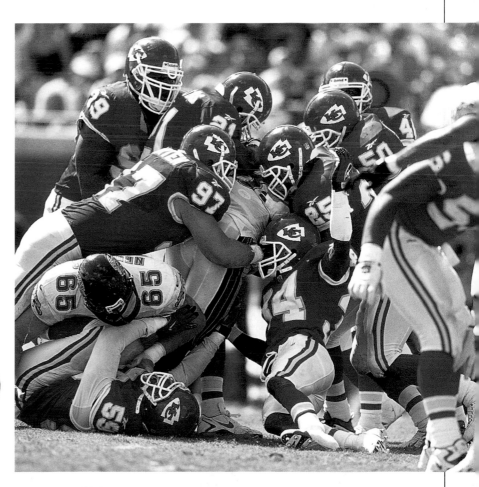

EIGHT AGAINST ONE

A good defence is like a swarm of very large bees. Swarming to the ball carrier like honey-starved insects, a defence, such as Kansas City's, above, can use sheer numbers to stop an offence in its tracks. A Jacksonville runner is somewhere in that sea of red.

Putting the Foot in Football

FOR MANY PEOPLE, THE NAME "AMERICAN FOOTBALL" is confusing. Only two players on an NFL team actually touch the ball with their feet, as opposed to football, where the game is based on footwork. But both sports have their roots in the same 19th-century English games, so the name of the American version of football makes historical sense. In fact, the first part of any player's body to touch the ball in every NFL game is the kicker's foot during the kickoff. Kickers also play a vital role on offence, providing scoring with field goals and extra points. A kicker who is accurate from long range gives his team a valuable weapon. Punters play a more defensive role, but one that is equally important. A long, accurate punt can pin an opponent deep in its own territory. And controlling territory is an important aspect of this game.

KICKOFF!
Before each half and after each score, one team kicks off to the other. The kicker places the football on a tee (above), and, after a running start (below) kicks the ball as far as he can downfield. The kicker's job is to kick the ball high and far, to give his team-mates time to get into position to make the tackle.

The holder positions the ball for the kicker.

A KICK IN 1.3 SECONDS

Jason Elam of the Broncos demonstrates the soccer style of kicking, used today by all NFL kickers. But before Elam can make this kick, the "center" must make a good snap, and the holder (16) must place the ball upright, with laces facing the target, and hold it there for Elam. Elam approaches from the side and swings his foot through the ball. All this must happen in about 1.3 seconds to avoid onrushing blockers. There is little room for mistakes in the kicking game.

BEST TOE FORWARD

Until soccer-style kickers came along in the 1960s, NFL kickers used a straight-ahead, toe-first style, here demonstrated by Mark Moseley, the NFL's last straight-ahead kicker.

DROP-KICKING

In the early days of the NFL, a strange hybrid of placekicking and punting was a big part of the game. "Dropkicks" were used to score field goals and extra points. NFL and Olympics legend Jim Thorpe (left) was a master of the art of dropping the ball on one end and kicking it just after the ball hit the ground.

The football was much rounder in the early NFL, making drop-kicks more accurate.

A RECORD KICK

Although born with half a right foot, Tom Dempsey set an NFL record with a 63-yard field goal with a straight-ahead motion in 1970. Jason Elam tied the mark in 1998.

Step 1: "Center" snaps ball 15 yards to punter.

Step 2: Punter cradles ball laces up and takes first step.

Step 4: Punter strikes ball with laces of shoe.

Step 3: Punter drops ball straight down and begins to swing leg.

THE ART OF PUNTING

Punting may look like one of the simplest football skills. But it actually is one of the hardest to master. Under the pressure of the opponents' rush, a punter must concentrate on the ball and punt it as far downfield as he can with as much accuracy as possible. Inconsistency is fatal for a punter.

Strategy

RUN OR PASS? GO LONG OR GO SHORT? To the left or the right? Play man-for-man or zone? Players and coaches face these questions and hundreds more during every NFL game, as every play presents dozens of options. Creating a successful football strategy is both a science and an art. The science is in the geometry of the playing field and the limits of the rules; the art comes in the creativity of using your eleven players in the best way possible. Football strategy is continually evolving, too, each new season and new coach bringing new ideas. The key parts of offensive strategy are plays and formations. Most teams use thick playbooks filled with hundreds of offensive plays. Each play can be run from a wide variety of formations. On defence, teams do not run plays; rather, they decide how they will set up in a given situation before the play starts. The genius of a coach is knowing when to use the right players for the right play from the right formation.

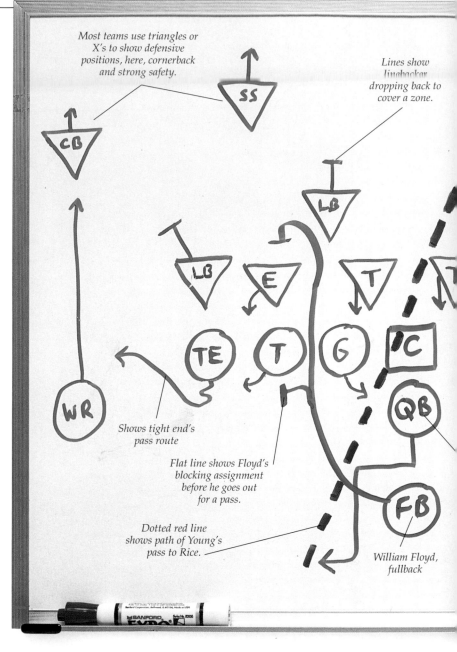

Most teams use triangles or X's to show defensive positions, here, cornerback and strong safety.

Lines show linebacker dropping back to cover a zone.

Shows tight end's pass route

Flat line shows Floyd's blocking assignment before he goes out for a pass.

Dotted red line shows path of Young's pass to Rice.

William Floyd, fullback

X's and O's, even in 1940

DIAGRAM OF A TOUCHDOWN
Above is a re-creation of an actual play diagram used by the 49ers to score the opening touchdown of Super Bowl XXIX. The play was called "Jet Left J.R.", and resulted in a 44-yard touchdown pass from Steve Young to Jerry Rice. The diagram is used by the team to show what each player's movement on the play should be. On the play, Young (QB) dropped back, faked a handoff to William Floyd (FB), rolled left, and threw a pass (red dotted line) to Rice (WR on right).

CHALK TALK
Using symbols unchanged for decades, NFL teams use play diagrams, whether on paper or a chalkboard, as part of their preparation for games. Shown drawing a play here is Green Bay's Hall of Fame coach Curly Lambeau.

Unbalanced line, with four players right of "center"

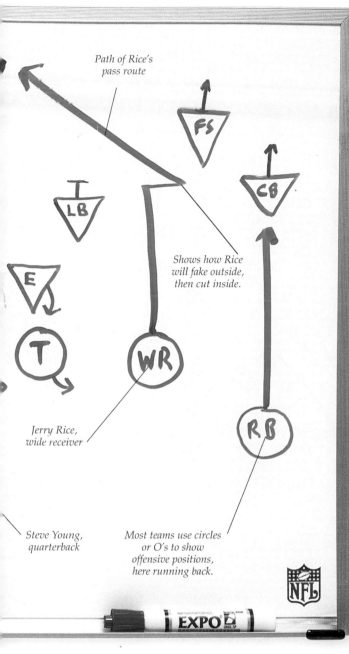

Path of Rice's pass route

FS

LB

CB

Shows how Rice will fake outside, then cut inside.

E

T

WR

RB

Jerry Rice, wide receiver

Steve Young, quarterback

Most teams use circles or O's to show offensive positions, here running back.

EXPO

NFL

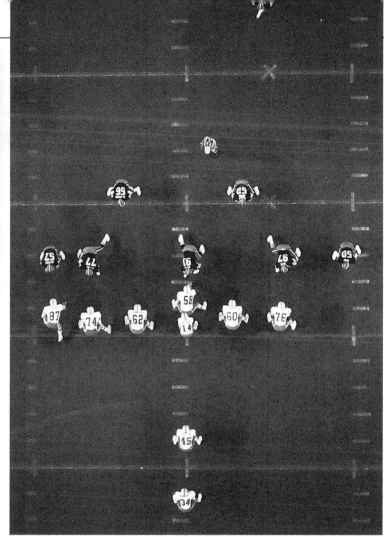

OVERHEAD VIEW
This overhead view (above) of an NFL game in progress shows the Oilers set up in a "Power-I" formation. The name comes from the arrangement of the two running backs behind the quarterback (two wide receivers are not shown). The Browns, on defence, will use their ends to "contain" the runners; the linebackers will fill holes on the line and react to the runners' direction. Talking football: The left side of this offensive formation is the "strong" side of the field, because that is where the tight end (87) is lined up.

GOOD OLD DAYS
Football formations have changed over time. While variations of the T-formation (above) have dominated for decades, the run-oriented Single-Wing offence (1934 Giants, below) dominated for many years.

SPECIAL TEAMS PLAYBOOKS
Most fans' attention is given to offensive and defensive strategies. But insiders know that special teams can play a vital part in a team's success. Players on the kickoff team (right), the punt-return squad, or the field-goal unit may not have as many plays to learn, but they can have just as much impact.

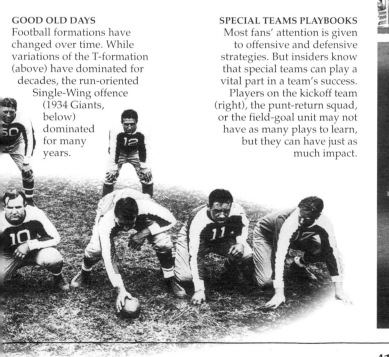

Locker Room

A LOCKER ROOM CAN BE A BORING place – just a room full of cubicles where players get dressed before playing a sport. But an NFL locker room on game day is anything but boring. Filled with players, coaches, trainers, equipment managers, and other team staff, a pre-game locker room is a beehive of activity. For players, the locker room is like a big clubhouse where they gather with their team-mates to prepare for the game. They dress and put on their game faces, they meet with coaches to go over last-minute instructions and strategy, or they spend a quiet moment by their locker before they go out into the roar of the crowd. After the game, the mood of the locker room depends on one thing: who won. There are few quieter places than a locker room after a loss. But there also are few more exciting places to be than an NFL locker room after a big win.

LAUNDRY DAY
One of the nice things about being an NFL player is that someone does your laundry for you. Equipment managers fill each player's locker with clean clothing – everything from socks (left) to jerseys – before every practice and game.

A chalkboard or white board for diagramming plays is a staple of NFL locker rooms.

Position coaches meet with players at halftime.

STRETCH IT OUT
Before a game, a locker room also can be a place to stretch out with the help of an athletic trainer. Usually, there is more than enough room for stretching exercises such as this one in the 49ers' locker room (left). Most NFL locker rooms are very large, with enough room for more than 50 players and coaches to dress for a game.

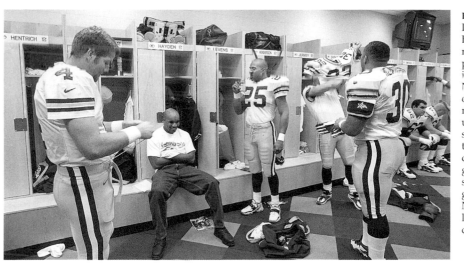

BEHIND THE SCENES
In this view of the Green Bay Packers' locker room, notice that each player has his own individual locker. Most NFL lockers have a tall open area for equipment managers to fill with uniforms, pads, and shoes, as well as room for the players' street clothes. A locking cabinet gives players a place to store valuables during games and practices. Notice, too, that NFL locker rooms are nicely carpeted.

TAKING FIVE
Locker rooms are a mix of public and private. Although players dress for games together, often the locker room is their final chance for a quiet moment before the game.

San Francisco's R.W. McQuarters uses music to get in the mood to play.

Players' lockers were much smaller in the old days.

METAL LOCKERS, CONCRETE FLOORS
The locker rooms of today's NFL players are luxurious, compared to earlier pro teams, as shown by this scene from the Los Angeles Dons' locker room in 1949. The Dons were part of the All-America Football Conference.

OKAY, GUYS, LISTEN UP!
A player uses the locker room three times on game day. Before and after the game it is a dressing and undressing room, but at halftime it is a classroom. Players meet with their coaches to go over what they did right and wrong in the first half, and what they need to do in the second half. Coaches often make key adjustments in strategy during halftime locker-room talks.

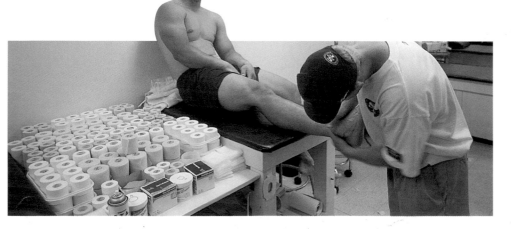

TAPE CITY
The trainer's room is located adjacent to the locker room. Here players are taped up before dressing. Superstitious players ask that they be taped with a fresh roll of tape each time.

Training Camp

THE SUPER BOWL DREAM BEGINS ANEW each July at NFL training camps. In the heat of summer, teams gather at sites across America to prepare for the upcoming season. The players meet new team-mates and, sometimes, new coaches. They lift weights, run through drills, learn new plays, and hone their bodies and minds for the coming season. Young players can earn a coveted place on the team or a disappointing ride back home. While veterans enjoy the renewal each training camp signifies, they usually don't feel the same way about the grueling two-a-day practice sessions. When they aren't practising, players spend many hours in the classroom, learning the plays their team will use in the coming season. And when camp ends before the final preseason game, the drive towards the Super Bowl begins for every player on every team.

Many training-camp drills are held without full pads.

WEIGHTY MATTERS
Strength is essential to success in football. Today, every team boasts a high-tech weight room – such as this one at the Bears' Halas Hall – filled with equipment players use to build up every part of their bodies.

FILL-IN FOOT
Machines such as this JUGS gun give passers and punters a rest. The two white wheels rotate at high speed to fling footballs downfield to receivers and punt returners.

TO-DO LIST
With just a month or so to get ready to play, teams create detailed daily plans, such as this step-by-step weightlifting list.

PILES OF PADS
During training camp, a wide variety of pads and pylons stand in for the obstacles players will face in games.

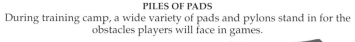

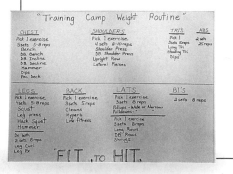

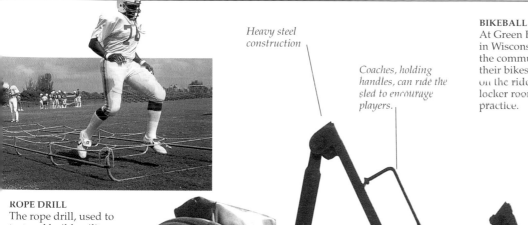

Heavy steel construction

Coaches, holding handles, can ride the sled to encourage players.

BIKEBALL
At Green Bay Packers camp in Wisconsin, kids from the community share their bikes with players on the ride back to the locker room after practice.

ROPE DRILL
The rope drill, used to test and build agility, has been a classic part of football training camps for decades. Players run through boxes formed by ropes – and try not to trip.

HIT IT!
The problem of how to practice hitting, blocking, and tackling without wearing out your teammates is solved with the blocking sled. Heavily padded, the sleds have smooth, flat bottoms so they can slide when pushed or hit. Weights can be added or removed to increase or decrease the difficulty of moving the sled.

Pads soften the impact on players.

OLDIE BUT GOODIE
Amid the high-tech equipment at NFL camps, some players prefer the old-fashioned medicine ball.

Smooth bottom allows sled to slide.

First Aid

prewrap   *tan athletic tape*   *cloth tape*   *gauze tape*

In a physical sport such as football, injuries are a part of the game. NFL teams are ready for any emergency with a staff of specialists and the latest in first aid and medical gear. Stadiums come equipped with X-ray machines for quick diagnosis; every team has a doctor on the sidelines for each game. The linchpin of an NFL team's medical staff is the athletic trainer. The trainer is a specialist who has undergone extensive training in college and in the field. The trainer is the person closest to the athletes, serving as their day-to-day resource for every problem from a headache to a knee injury. A trainer monitors the entire team for any problems, deals rapidly with on-field injuries, and oversees rehabilitation after an injury. In addition, he works with players to prepare for games and practices to avoid injuries as much as possible. With years of training and trunks full of equipment, an NFL trainer is ready for anything that might happen. But he always is happiest when nothing does.

Bag with first-aid equipment

A trainer's number-one tool: athletic tape

Additional rolls of various tapes

READY FOR WORK
On game day, NFL trainers, such as San Diego's James Collins (left), dress in comfortable, team-identified clothes. Trainers may have to run onto the field or to the locker room to aid a player, or they may have to help lead or carry players off the field; a suit and tie won't do.

Replacement mouth guard

Tape scissors

Ever-present athletic tape

Sunscreen

SAFE KNEE
Some players, including many linemen, now wear strap-on knee braces, such as these, under their socks and trousers as a preventive measure. Trainers help players choose such equipment.

white athletic tape

Ace bandage

TAPE'S ROLE
Trainers use miles of various kinds of tapes and wraps during a season. Most players use tape to support some part of their body for every game and practice.

SPORTS SCIENCE
To help players recover from injuries, or from the bumps and bruises of a typical game, some trainers use a combination ultrasound/electrostimulator machine such as this one. The power of sound waves and low-voltage electricity helps ease muscle pain.

Finger splints

Scissors for removing facemask clips

Cord for electrostimulator function

Sticky pads help hold electrodes in place.

Silver head of ultrasound wand is rubbed over affected area.

Eyewash

Liquid makes removing sticky tape from skin easier.

THE WATERBOYS
One of the duties of most assistant trainers is to provide players with water or sports drinks on the sideline and during time outs. Teams also hire additional workers on game days to help with this important function. Trainers oversee the hydration of players during practice, workouts, and games.

STRETCH SUPPORT
Under a trainer's or doctor's supervision, players recovering from knee injuries may wear a stretchable rubber or neoprene sleeve such as this one. This sleeve gives the knee support while letting the player exercise the injured knee back into shape.

BLACK BAG
NFL trainers fill trunks and large cases with equipment. But many trainers also keep a smaller bag handy with often-used equipment. They also can carry this bag out to a practice field or during pre-game warmups. The bag contains the smaller, day-to-day items a trainer uses to deal with minor problems or to supply quick fixes that help players get safely back into the action.

Rubber gloves

GETTING BETTER
One of a trainer's most important jobs is helping players recover from injuries. Trainers show players how to properly use equipment such as ankle weights (left) or rubber cords (right) to successfully complete rehabilitation.

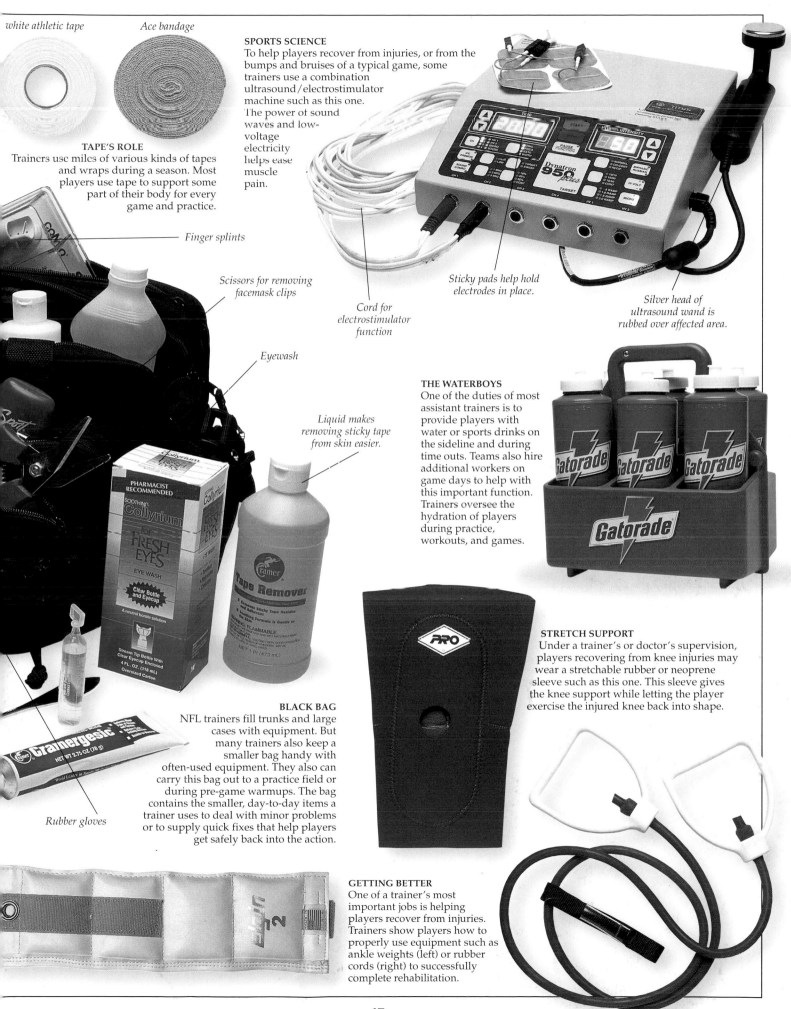

On the Sidelines

To fans in the stands or to those watching on television, the sidelines of an NFL game must look like chaos. But what looks at times like a disorganized mob actually is a well-ordered group. While a fortunate few of the people on the sidelines are just spectators with a close-up view of the action, the vast majority are hard at work. It takes dozens of people to make an NFL game happen, from chain-crew members to stadium staff to security. The geography of a sideline does not vary much from stadium to stadium. The bench area is a clearly marked rectangle between the 35-yard lines. The chain crews roam the sidelines nearest the action. So do photographers. Like everyone alongside the playing field, they all must always be ready to move – quickly – when the action spills over onto the sidelines.

Marker shows start of offensive drive.

Down marker

DIAL-A-DOWN

Six-foot-wide sideline area

Poles have rubber tips for safety.

SHOOTERS
Dozens of photographers cover every NFL game. Their sideline spots are among the most coveted in sports journalism. NFL photographers typically use fine-grain, slow-speed film and extra-long lenses to capture the fast-moving, distant action. After a score or when a team crosses mid-field, photographers often pick up their gear and run to the other end of the field to catch up to the action.

READY FOR ACTION
NFL teams use huge bags of ice and gallons of water and sports drinks during games. Trainers keep it all handy, usually behind or at the end of a team's bench. Ice is placed into smaller bags to make icepacks for minor injuries. NFL players get all the water they need to stay hydrated.

Pom-pons in
team colours

**CAN YOU
SIGN THIS,
PLEASE?**
While most NFL
teams have too much
to do on game days
during the regular
season to sign
autographs at the
stadium, the sidelines
at training camp
sometimes are a great
place to meet heroes
and get signatures.

THE CHAIN GANG
Dressed in their
official uniforms with
distinctive striped
vests, the "chain
gang" works with
sideline officials to
keep track of downs,
the spot of the ball,
and distance to the
first down. One
member mans the
down marker, while
two more members
hold each end of the
10-yard chain used to
measure first downs.

*Chain crew
members have
uniforms, too.*

*Orange pads make
poles easy for fans
and players to spot.*

*Water botttles for
use on field during
time outs*

PART OF THE JOB
No matter what the
weather, the chain-crew
members must stand at
their posts. Amid this
snowstorm at a
Pittsburgh Steelers
game, this first-down
chain marker holder
remains ready for
action. Crew members
run on to the field with
their chain when
directed by officials to
help measure whether
a team has made a
first down.

SIS, BOOM, BAH!
Cheerleaders and
high-energy dance teams
have become as much a part
of today's NFL sideline
action as the chain gang.
Almost every team has some
sort of group that dances,
leads cheers, and encourages
the fans. Some perform at
halftime as well, and stars
from each squad make the trip
to the Super Bowl and the Pro
Bowl. Many teams' cheerleaders
also make visits to charities in
their local communities, as
well as appear at other
team functions.

HANGING OUT
A trio of 49ers –
Jerry Rice, Terrell
Owens, and Steve
Young – relax in the
moments before a
game. Teams use the
benches to rest when
not in the action and
to meet with
their coaches to plot
strategy.

Keeping Order

AMERICAN FOOTBALL, LIKE EVERY OTHER SPORT, HAS RULES. During NFL games, seven on-field officials make sure those rules are obeyed. The first NFL games only had three officials. Beginning in 1929, additional officials were added periodically until the total reached its current level in 1978. The referee is the chief official; not only is he in charge of the crew of officials, but also he signals penalties to the fans and the teams by using hand signals and a microphone. The other officials are the umpire, the head linesman, and the line, field, side, and back judges. Each man patrols a specific area of the field to watch for certain penalties. However, just as players do, officials work as a team and often help out in another official's area. Officials undergo many years of testing and evaluation before reaching the NFL, and constantly are monitored to ensure that their performance is of the highest caliber. It is not an easy job keeping 22 large, fast-moving men in order, but NFL officials are the best in the business.

A wrist strap connected to a string worn around the fingers helps officials keep track of downs and ball position.

Whistle

U 110

Bean bag

PRE-POLYESTER
NFL official Jack Reader modelled the officials' uniform in style when he first took the field in 1961. Long sleeves were worn in all weather, while the bow tie gave an air of formality to the outfit.

FLAG ON THE PLAY
This bright-yellow penalty marker, called a penalty flag, is thrown by an official when he spots a foul. Officials fill the end of the flag with unpopped popcorn to help it gain altitude and return to the field.

FUMBLE!
An official will throw this small bean bag to the ground at the spot of a fumble or interception to signal a turnover. Play may continue, and the bean bag is recovered later. Along with confirming a turnover, the location helps calculate the distance of any return of the turnover. The number on the bean bag identifies the official who threw it.

U 110

LAWMAN
Umpire Ron Botchan, a former player for the Chargers and Oilers, raises his hand and blows his whistle to stop play after a tackle. The umpire takes his position on the field directly behind the defensive line and must be nimble to avoid contact.

holding   offside   illegal motion   first down   safety   touchdown, successful field goal or extra point

Like players, officials wear unique numbers. Letters (U for umpire here) indicate their job titles.

SIGNAL ACHIEVEMENTS

After a foul has been committed, the referee uses one of more than 30 hand signals to describe the penalty to the stadium and television audience. In addition to using hand signals, the referee wears a wireless microphone to announce other information, such as the penalty in yards or downs and the number of the player who committed the foul. Hand signals also are used to signify successful scoring plays – touchdowns, field goals, extra points, and safeties.

Some officials carry their penalty flag in their belts, others in their back pockets.

Officials record basic game and team information here.

UMPIRE'S
NFL OFFICIAL GAME CARD   NFL

WARN:
LEAVE:
VISITORS:
TEAM COLOR

PUNT

FGA

TRY

This card is used by umpires to track players on special teams.

PAPERWORK

All officials record the fouls they call on special cards provided by the league. After each game, officials submit reports to the NFL office on fouls called. In addition, each crew of officials is graded and meets weekly to review their performance during their previous game.

PEACEMAKER

Football can be a game of raw emotion. Armed only with their authority, a loud whistle, and the threat of a penalty flag, officials occasionally must step between warring players.

Fabulous Fans

EVERY SPORT HAS FANS, BUT FANS OF NFL FOOTBALL are a special breed. Perhaps no other sport generates greater passion, loyalty, enthusiasm, and artistic creativity (see painted faces at right). Fans are a part of every NFL game whether they are in the stadium on game day, at home watching on television, or dissecting plays on Monday morning. NFL fans participate in their favourite game in dozens of ways. Attending "tailgate parties" or spreading a bounty of Sunday snacks over the coffee table; playing touch football in the car park or the back garden; pulling on treasured jerseys or team sweatshirts to watch the game; all this is part of an NFL fan's game day. By any measure, this passion for the game has made the NFL America's most popular sport for many years.

He has eyes only for Miami.

Buttons, buttons, and more buttons

Hand-painted jersey

FOOTBALL: A FAMILY AFFAIR
Few things are as cool as sharing a Jaguars "ROOOARRR!" at a game with your son . . . or with your dad. Loyalty for an NFL team is one that is passed down through generations, even for a team as new as Jacksonville, which joined the NFL in 1995.

FAMILY OF FANS
These fans were among the more than 19 million people who attended NFL games during the 1998 regular season and postseason. More than 100 million people watch an NFL game on television each Sunday.

PAINT AND PIGSKIN
As shown by this array of artistic fans, wearing a jersey with the team logo just isn't enough. Putting their best face forward, fans use their favourite team's colours as the palette to create their own version of a game face.

TAILGATE!
Whether sausages in Green Bay (right), nachos in San Diego, or barbecue in Kansas City, pre-game tailgate food is as much a part of an NFL game day as the pre-game singing of the National Anthem.

FIVE CHEERS FOR . . .
. . . the Washington Hogettes. Named for a powerful Redskins offensive line of the 1980s, this quintet of strangely dressed fans is one of the NFL's most durable and well-known. In 1999, they joined 30 other fans or groups of fans as members of a special fans' wing of the Pro Football Hall of Fame.

DRESS THE PART
This San Francisco 49ers vendor displays just a handful of the many items fans can buy to display their team loyalty. While many fans buy new gear each season, others retain cherished – and lucky – hats, shirts, and jackets season after season.

NFL Stadiums

EARLY IN THE 1920s, FANS OFTEN DID NOT have stadiums in which to watch games, only empty fields with playing areas. And in the beginning, NFL stadiums were a far cry from the high-tech stadiums that fans and teams enjoy today. Many early NFL teams often played in small college stadiums, or in huge baseball parks. Today, many NFL teams play in new state-of-the-art stadiums. Some of the newer facilities include those in Cleveland, Washington, D.C., Tampa Bay, Carolina, and Jacksonville. Along with NFL action, these new stadiums provide luxury boxes, in-seat video screens, an array of food and drink, exhibits of memorabilia, and even football theme parks. A century after football took root in America, the field remains the focus. But today, what surrounds the field is special, too.

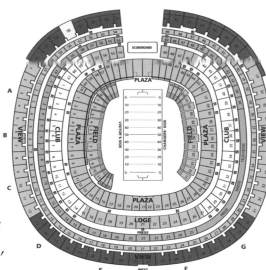

WHERE'S YOUR SEAT?
Stadium maps help fans find their seats. This map of San Diego's Qualcomm Stadium shows the field, the "club" seats in white, the "plaza" and "view" seats in green, and the luxury boxes, team offices, and the press box in orange. Stadium entrance gates are shown by letters around the outside of the map.

HAVE A SEAT
Many stadiums, especially newer ones, sport seats in an array of team colours. Some stadiums also offer special club seat areas, as well as luxury boxes with chairs and sofas.

Large towers atop stadiums provide light for night games or on overcast days.

Panther statue weighs 3,000 pounds.

OUTDOOR STADIUMS
For many teams, their stadium is a shrine to their team's legacy and history. Some teams, including the Carolina Panthers, add to the ambiance of their stadiums by placing statues outside to honour their team or its players, coaches, or owners.

The heavy fabric roof of the Metrodome is supported by air pressure.

SAIL HO!

At many NFL stadiums, the game is just part of the fun. Along with exhibits of American football gear and memorabilia, some stadiums offer extras such as Tampa Bay's pirate ship below. Located above the end zone seats, the ship "fires" its cannons when the Buccaneers score, and cheerleaders and fans can dance on its decks. Some teams have set up NFL Experience football theme parks outside their stadiums. Fans can visit them before the game and take part in special football activities.

INDOOR FOOTBALL

Since the 1960s, new technologies have helped create massive domed stadiums, so that teams can enjoy perfect weather all year-round. Seven NFL teams play in domed stadiums, including the Vikings, who play in the Metrodome (above).

View of downtown Charlotte rises above the stadium.

Capacity at Carolina's Ericsson Stadium is 73,250.

Giant video screens offer fans instant replay and the latest statistics.

TV GUIDE

Another way fans are entertained during NFL games is via the enormous video screens located near the scoreboards. These screens show replays of the game fans are watching and highlights from other games, as well as special video features created by the teams.

Best seat in the house? Many fans feel that the 50-yard line is the best place to sit.

FULL HOUSE

These fans at Ericsson Stadium were among the more than 15 million fans who attended NFL games during the 1998 regular season, the second time the league has topped that attendance mark. Also in 1998, NFL teams averaged an all-time record of more than 64,000 fans per game. NFL tickets are some of the hardest to get in sports, with stadiums averaging better than 90 per cent of capacity.

In Any Weather

NFL PLAYERS WOULD MAKE GREAT POSTMEN. Like letter carriers, players let neither rain, nor snow, nor sleet (nor anything else) stop them from their appointed games. In the 80-season history of the NFL, no regular-season or postseason game has been cancelled because of weather. (A few pre-season games have been postponed or shortened because of thunderstorms.) NFL players – and fans, too, for that matter – stick it out no matter what Mother Nature threws at them. Games have been played in driving rainstorms, in blizzards, and on fields so thick with mud that players on both teams seemed to be wearing the same colors. Games go on whether the temperature is freezing or steaming. Let baseball have its rainouts. In the NFL, the game must go on.

COLD QUARTERBACKS
All players are affected by cold weather, but none more so than quarterbacks, who must pass and hand off a frigid ball with frozen fingers. In such games, many passers use padded hand warmers (left) to keep the chill off their fingers between plays. Receivers and running backs usually rely on gloves.

TWO FACES OF MUD
Playing in mud is fun if you win; it is not if you don't. Witness happy Aaron Taylor of the Packers (left) and sad Dana Stubblefield of the 49ers. Guess which team won their teams' muddy 1996 NFL playoff game.

CHILLY CHAMPIONSHIP
In the 1948 NFL Championship Game, played in a raging blizzard in Philadelphia, the Eagles (above) threw off their sideline coats and came off their bench long enough to defeat the Chicago Cardinals 7-0.

PLANNING A-HEAD
While players can bundle up against winter's freezing temperatures (Buffalo punter Chris Mohr, right), there was not much the Eagles and Bears (left) could do to prepare for a thick fog that descended at halftime of their 1988 playoff game. Chicago muddled through to win the game known since as "The Fog Bowl".

RAIN, RAIN . . . SO WHAT?
What happens when it rains on an NFL game? The players get wet. Chris Chandler of the Falcons barely can be seen through the downpour during this 1997 game at normally sunny San Diego. The only concession to heavy rain is made by officials who attempt to use dry footballs as much as possible.

TRUE FANS
The only way to tell the players is with...a hose? For this 1964 game in St. Louis, nearly 30,000 fans braved a pre-game storm that dumped more than an inch of rain in an hour to watch the Giants and Cardinals battle to a 10-10 tie. Perhaps the only winner that day was Mother Nature.

THE ICE BOWL
The coldest NFL game ever was the 1967 NFL Championship Game. The Packers defeated the Cowboys (below) 21-17 in Green Bay. Game-time temperature was -25º C (-13º F) with a wind-chill factor of -45º C (-48º F).

Football on TV

THE FIRST NFL GAME TO BE TELEVISED WAS PLAYED IN 1939; the first coast-to-coast broadcast of the championship game occurred in 1951. But in 1958, millions of Americans watched as the Baltimore Colts defeated the New York Giants in the first overtime championship game. That watershed event cemented the bond between the NFL and television forever. Through the years, NFL football has become one of the perennial powerhouses of television. Every NFL game is televised in at least part of the United States. Each season, more countries around the world join the list of those receiving NFL telecasts. Since 1984, the Super Bowl annually has been the top-rated television show of any kind. And of the top 20 most-watched sporting events since 1961, 18 are NFL games, including 17 Super Bowls. The NFL works with television and radio network partners to bring hundreds of millions of fans the thrill of NFL action.

GOALPOST-CAM
Smaller and smaller cameras are taking viewers into more places than ever, as well as providing unusual views of the action. This remote camera rests atop the support arm of the goal post and can be turned to follow the flight of a field-goal or extra-point attempt through the uprights.

Headset connects camera operator to control booth

Protective frame for camera operator

Camera lens casing

SOUNDS OF THE GAME
Modern sound equipment has brought the sounds of the game into viewers' living rooms. Networks station several of these parabolic microphones around the field to capture the voices of the players and coaches and the sounds of colliding pads and helmets.

Parabolic microphones

Platform raises and lowers to follow action.

Dolly arm is controlled by a technician on the ground.

HELLO, DOLLY
The most-seen angle on NFL broadcasts comes from this dolly-mounted camera that rolls along the sideline behind the benches, following the action on the field. The dolly can cover the length of the field, as well as be raised or lowered to provide different viewpoints.

58

IN THE STUDIO
All of the NFL's network partners provide in-depth coverage of the league through game coverage and studio shows. FOX Sports (right), CBS Sports, ABC Sports, and ESPN were NFL broadcast partners in 1999.

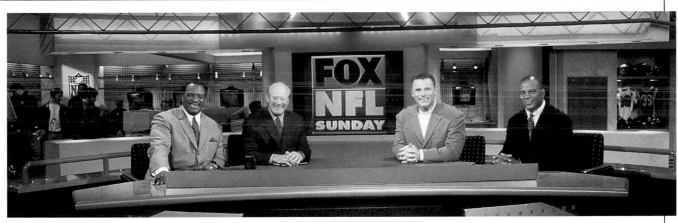

Pilot and camera operator ride in gondola below blimp.

LOOK! UP IN THE SKY!
Perhaps the quintessential view of a football game comes from the blimps that circle over NFL games. These dramatic overhead shots capture the entire stadium, as well as give unique views of the action.

Fluorescent orange gloves make this television official easy to spot.

A bright green hat is worn by the official making sure enough time outs are taken.

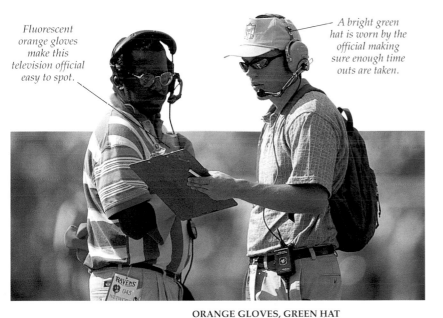

WIRED
This tangle of wires is just from one truck at one game. For every NFL broadcast, networks string miles of cable and wire from control trucks to cameras inside the stadium.

KEEPERS OF THE FLAME
The camera operators, writers, editors, and producers at NFL Films have captured every moment of NFL action for nearly 40 years. NFL Films' unique, dramatic style perfectly captures the drama, humour, power, and thrill of the NFL. Each season, Films photographers shoot miles of film to create dozens of Emmy-winning videos for fans to enjoy.

ORANGE GLOVES, GREEN HAT
During NFL games, the referee looks for a pair of bright orange gloves signalling on the sideline for an official time out. The "green hat" official also ensures that an NFL broadcast runs smoothly and that the correct breaks are taken.

NFL Films uses real film, not videotape, in its cameras.

The Super Bowl

THE NFL'S ANNUAL CHAMPIONSHIP GAME is more than just a contest between the champions of the AFC and the NFC. Since the first game following the 1966 season, the Super Bowl has evolved into the largest single-day sporting event in the world. More than 800 million people in more than 180 countries watched Super Bowl XXXIII from Miami. Visitors from all over the world gather in the Super Bowl host city to experience the action, even if they do not have one of the most coveted tickets in sports. While the action on the field remains the centrepiece, a virtual circus of events surrounds the game – from pre-game parties to concerts to charity events to The NFL Experience theme park. But while fans gather pennants, hats, T-shirts, towels, and key rings to take home along with their memories, the players all want to take home two things: the Vince Lombardi Trophy, which is awarded to the Super Bowl champion, and the one-of-a-kind Super Bowl rings given to each player on the winning team.

Laces ar and for by hand

The football on the trophy is exactly the size of the official game ball.

SUNDAY, JANUARY 26, 1997
SUPER BOWL XXXI
NEW ORLEANS, LOUISIANA • SUPERDOME

SUPER FLAGS
Pennants, which are so symbolic as a football souvenir, have their roots in brightly coloured ribbons worn by early football players in the days before uniforms. Fans of each team would wave scarves of the same colour as their favourite team. Tied to sticks, the scarves became pennants.

SUPER RINGS
Each winning team creates a unique design for a ring given to all its team members, coaches, and staff. The design usually incorporates the team name and logo and the NFL shield, and usually includes a host of diamonds. Each ring can cost no more than $5,000 (£3,125). These rings are from Super Bowls I, XVIII, and XXXII.

SUPER TIME
Until Super Bowl XXV, the man named most valuable player in the Super Bowl received this one-of-a-kind watch. Today he receives the Pete Rozelle Trophy.

MOST VALUABLE PLAYER
SUPER BOWL IX
FRANCO HARRIS

SUPER TROPHY
Crafted by Tiffany & Co. from sterling silver, the Vince Lombardi Trophy is awarded to the winning Super Bowl team. Lombardi coached the Green Bay Packers to victories in the first two Super Bowls. The 7-pound, 21-inch trophy was designed by Tiffany's Oscar Reidener in 1966, and consists of an actual-size silver football atop a triangular base.

VINCE LOMBARDI TROPHY

NFL

SUPER STUFF TO WEAR

The moment the two Super Bowl teams are determined, presses roll, churning out T-shirts, hats, sweatshirts, and more, depicting the two teams' helmets and logos. The same happens again after the game, with merchandise showing the winning team and score. Thanks to a little pre-planning, the winning team dons its championship caps as the final gun goes off to end the game.

SUPER TICKETS

The most-coveted piece of cardboard in sports is a ticket to the Super Bowl. Strangely, tickets to the first game (top) did not sell out. Every game since has, however. To foil counterfeiters hoping to cash in on the prize, the NFL incorporates a number of security devices into the tickets. In the past, these have included holograms, special inks, infrared stamps, and special paper. After the game, the ticket stub becomes a valuable collectible as well.

SUPER PROGRAMME

The annual *Official Super Bowl Game Programme* is one of the most popular collectibles at the game. The cover is illustrated with "theme art" that also appears on posters and many other items throughout the Super Bowl city. Sold at the stadium and around the nation, the program is completed the night the two teams are determined.

SUPER FANS

Without fans, there would be no Super Bowl paraphernalia. Fans of the two Super Bowl teams snap up hundreds of items featuring their team's logo. The Super Bowl is a multi-million pound event for licensed merchandise.

SUPER SOUVENIRS

Among the hundreds of Super Bowl souvenirs available each year are mugs, pens, calendars, dolls, key chains, numberplate holders, flags, pillowcases, earrings, playing cards, stuffed animals, golf balls, neckties, windbreakers, and, of course, an endless variety of T-shirts.

Super Bowl Action

From the first day of training camp in the heat of summer through afternoons in the icy winds of winter, every NFL season boils down to the ultimate day: Super Bowl Sunday. On that Sunday each year in late January, heroes are born, legends are made, champions are forged. The events of Super Bowl Sundays past are the touchstones in the collective memories – good and bad – of NFL fans. Some of those memories can be invoked with only a name: Lombardi, Namath, Bradshaw, Montana, Marcus, "The Fridge". Some merely with the Roman numeral that identifies each Super Bowl: III, XX, XXXII. With a world full of fans watching, a lifetime of effort by players and coaches can pay off or be buried in a flash. Win or lose, new memories are made to remain fresh and vital until the next Super Bowl rolls around.

Bart Starr later coached Green Bay from 1975-1983.

SUPER STEELERS
Led by quarterback Terry Bradshaw (above) and the "Steel Curtain" defence, the Pittsburgh Steelers became the first team to win four Super Bowls (IX, X, XIII, and XIV). Since then, the 49ers and Cowboys each have passed Pittsburgh with five Super Bowl victories apiece.

STARR OF THE SUPER BOWL
After winning their fourth and fifth NFL championships of the decade in 1966 and 1967, the Green Bay Packers defeated the American Football League champions (Chiefs and Raiders, respectively) in the first two Super Bowls. During the first three years, the game was known as the AFL-NFL World Championship Game, but by the third, it was popularly known as the Super Bowl.

MAGIC MARCUS
A Super Bowl-record 74-yard touchdown run by most valuable player Marcus Allen in Super Bowl XVIII was the highlight of the Raiders' third Super Bowl championships in eight years.

PERFECT SEASON
The Miami Dolphins capped off the only perfect season in NFL history with a 14-7 victory over Washington in Super Bowl VII. Miami relied on its tough "No-Name Defence" and the running of Larry Csonka (above) and Jim Kiick to finish the season undefeated and untied at 17-0. The following season, the Dolphins made it two titles in a row, winning Super Bowl VIII.

SAN FRANCISCO TREAT
In Super Bowl XXIII, superstar wide receiver Jerry Rice caught 11 passes for a Super Bowl record 215 yards to earn most-valuable-player honours and help the 49ers win the third of their five Super Bowl championships.

DREAM COME TRUE
This is the moment every NFL player dreams about: when he holds aloft the Vince Lombardi Trophy as the NFL champion. Denver quarterback John Elway flashes the smile of a man whose dream has come true – again – after Denver's Super Bowl XXXIII victory, its second in two seasons.

WIDE RIGHT
Buffalo Bills kicker Scott Norwood (11) watches as his potential game-winning 47-yard field-goal attempt sails wide right in Super Bowl XXV, preserving the Giants' 20-19 victory.

THE FRIDGE
With this spike after scoring on a short run in Chicago's 46-10 victory in Super Bowl XX, defensive tackle William (Refrigerator) Perry put an exclamation point on the Bears' magical 1985 season. During the team's dominating 15-1 regular season, Perry captured the nation's fancy as a rotund rookie with an infectious grin who was sometimes put in to run on goal-line plays.

Index

Acknowledgments

DK Eyewitness Football was produced by the Publishing Group of NFL Properties, Inc.

National Football League Properties, Inc.
Publishing Group
6701 Center Drive West, Suite 1111
Los Angeles, California 90045

www.nfl.com

Editor-in-Chief: John Wiebusch. General Manager: Bill Barron. Managing Editor: Chuck Garrity, Sr.
Eyewitness Football Editor: James Buckley, Jr. *Eyewitness Football* Art Director: Bill Madrid. Director-Photo Services: Paul Spinelli. Photo Editor: Kevin Terrell. Manager-Photo Services: Tina Resnick. Director-Manufacturing:
Dick Falk. Director-Print Services: Tina Dahl. Manager-Computer Graphics: Sandra Gordon. Publishing Director: Bob O'Keefe. Publishing Manager: Lori Quenneville.

The editors and designers of NFL Publishing would like the thank the following people and organizations for their assistance in creating *Eyewitness Football*: Pete Fierle, Pro Football Hall of Fame; Kirk Reynolds and Kevin Lartigue, San Francisco 49ers; James Collins, San Diego Chargers; Professional Football Athletic Trainers' Society; Wilson Sporting Goods Co.; Riddell Co.; Logo Athletic; Champion Sports; Vance McDaniel; Ron Botchan, NFL umpire.

Photography Credits

Cover
Michael Burr/NFLP (7), Joe Culliton, Tracy Frankel, NFL Photos , John H. Reid, George Rose, Tony Tomsic
Pages 6-7
NFL Photos (all)
Pages 8-9
NFL Photos (8), Pro Football Hall of Fame
Pages 10-11
Peter Brouillet, NFL Photos (2), Darryl Norenberg, Rich Pilling, Robert Riger, United Press, Michael Zagaris
Pages 12-13
Michael Burr/NFLP (5), Pro Football Hall of Fame, Wide World Photos
Pages 14-15
Camera Work, Chris Covatta, Brian Drake, Allen Kee, NFL Photos (2), Frank Rippon, Bob Rosato, James D. Smith, Jim Turner
Pages 16-17
David Boss, NFL Photos, Louis Raynor, Paul Spinelli/NFLP, Baron Wolman

Pages 18-19
Eric Lars Bakke, Michael Burr/NFLP, Joe Culliton, Gerald Gallegos, Ross Lewis, Joe Patronite, Bill Wood
Pages 20-21
Paul Masturzo, John McDonough, Al Messerschmidt (2), Darrell Sandler, Mike Solari, Tony Tomsic, Greg Trott
Pages 22-23
James Biever, Michael Burr/NFLP (2), Dorling Kindersley (3), Ross Lewis (2), NFL Photos, Courtesy: Riddell Company
Pages 24-25
Peter Brouillet, Malcolm Emmons, Glenn James, Ross Lewis, Al Messerschmidt, Frank Rippon, Fred Roe, Bob Rosato, James D. Smith
Pages 26-27
James Biever, Michael Burr/NFLP (6), NFL Photos (2)
Pages 28-29
Michael Burr/NFLP (2), Merv Corning, Bob Holt/St. Louis Post-Dispatch, NFL Photos (2)

Pages 30-31
Michael Burr/NFLP (7), Bob Ewell
Pages 32-33
Henry Barr Studios, Peter Brouillet, Michael Burr/NFLP (2), NFL Photos
Pages 34-35
Peter Brouillet, Scott Cunningham, Allen Kee, Bernie Nuñez, David Stluka, Mitchell Reibel, Robert Skeoch, Paul Spinelli/NFLP, Jim Turner
Pages 36-37
Al Messerschmidt, NFL Photos, James D. Smith, John Reid, Bob Rosato, Michael Zagaris
Pages 38-39
NFL Photos (2), Rich Pilling, Joe Robbins, Paul Spinelli/NFLP, David Stluka (3), Ron Vesely (2)
Pages 40-41
Michael Burr/NFLP, Al Messerschmidt, NFL Photos, Pro Football Hall of Fame, Kevin Terrell/NFLP
Pages 42-43
James Biever, Michael Burr/NFLP, NFL Photos, Michael Zagaris (4)

Pages 44-45
Jonathan Daniel, David Drapkin, Al Messerschmidt (3), Mitchell Reibel, Steve Woltmann, Michael Zagaris
Pages 46-47
Michael Burr/NFLP (all)
Pages 48-49
Tracy Frankel, Mitchell Reibel, Bob Rosato (2), G.B. Rose, Thom Vollenweider, Michael Zagaris
Pages 50-51
Michael Burr/NFLP (4), Michael Conroy, David Drapkin, Paul Jasienski, Greg LeBouef, NFL Photos, Paul Spinelli/NFLP (3)
Pages 52-53
David Drapkin, Tracy Frankel, Gerald Gallegos, Allen Kee (2), John McDonough, Steven Murphy (2), Paul Spinelli/NFLP (2), Allen Dean Steele (2), David Stluka
Pages 54-55
Greg Crisp (2), Allen Kee, R.A. Kolodziej, Lara Sahakian, David Stluka

Pages 56-57
David Drapkin, Malcolm Emmons, Al Messerschmidt, Pro Football Hall of Fame, Joe Robbins, Bob Rosato, Paul Spinelli/NFLP, Herb Weitman, Michael Zagaris
Pages 58-59
Michael Burr/NFLP, Bruce Dierdorf, FOX Sports, Tracy Frankel, Chris Schwenk, Paul Spinelli/NFLP, John H. Reid, G.B. Rose
Pages 60-61
Michael Burr/NFLP (4), Courtesy: Logo Athletic, NFL Photos (10)
Pages 62-63
David Boss, Bill Cummings, Scott Cunningham, James Flores, Al Messerschmidt, Rich Pilling, Manny Rubio, David Stluka

DK Publishing books are available at special discounts for bulk purchases for sales promotions or premiums. Special editions, including personalized covers, excerpts of existing guides, and corporate imprints can be created in large quantities for specific needs. For more information, contact Special Markets Dept./DK Publishing, Inc., 95 Madison Ave., New York, NY 10016. FAX: 1-800-600-9098.